Boreout!

Boreout! is the result of a special collaboration between Kogan Page and Redline Wirtschaft, and imprint of Finanzbuch Verlag GmbH, Germany's leading publisher. Selected best-selling titles previously published by Redline Wirtschaft are translated into English and published by Kogan Page to ensure a worldwide distribution.

Boreout!

Overcoming workplace demotivation

Philippe Rothlin & Peter Werder

**KOGAN
PAGE**

London and Philadelphia

For Bianca. For Nicole.

Originally published in 2007 in Germany as *Diagnose Boreout* by Redline Wirtschaft, FinanzBuch Verlag GmbH, Munich, Germany www.finanzbuchverlag.de

First published in Great Britain and the United States in 2008 by Kogan Page Limited

120 Pentonville Road
London N1 9JN
United Kingdom
www.koganpage.com

525 South 4th Street, #241
Philadelphia PA 19147
USA

© Redline Wirtschaft, FinanzBuch Verlag, Munich, Germany, 2007, 2008

The right of Philippe Rothlin and Peter R Werder to be identified as the authors of this work has been asserted by them in accordance with the Copyright, Designs and Patents Act 1988.

ISBN 978 0 7494 5339 8

British Library Cataloguing-in-Publication Data

A CIP record for this book is available from the British Library.

Library of Congress Cataloging-in-Publication Data

Rothlin, Philippe.
    Boreout! : overcoming workplace demotivation / Philippe Rothlin and Peter R. Werder.
      p. cm.
    Includes bibliographicl references and index.
    ISBN 978-0-7494-5339-8
  1. Employee motivation. 2. Job satisfaction. 3. Performance. I. Werder, Peter R. II. Title.
    HF5549.5.M63R68 2008
    658.3'14—dc22

2008017776

Typeset by JS Typesetting Ltd, Porthcawl, Mid Glamorgan
Printed and bound in India by Replika Press Pvt Ltd

Contents

Figures and tables

FIGURES

TABLES

About the authors

Philippe Rothlin studied law and business administration at the University of St Gallen and holds an MBA from ESADE Business School. He has been working as a project manager in the banking sector for many years. He is co-founder of the advertising agency Greutzi, headquartered in Barcelona, Spain and works as a business strategy consultant.

Peter R Werder studied journalism, philosophy and musicology at the University of Zurich. He took his doctorate degree in philosophy. He has worked as a journalist and public relations business consultant for many years. He is now in charge of the communications department of a large company in Switzerland.

About the authors

Acknowledgements

Part of writing is researching, collecting, observing – and above all a constant exchange of views with people who could make a contribution for the most varied of reasons. At this point we give general thanks to all those who critically scrutinized our theory again and again, and finally read our manuscript with careful eyes. We especially thank Pascal Bollier and Achim Kuhn, with whom we have had hours of discussions about boreout as well as about the book itself.

We would like to thank all those people who in countless conversations have not only confirmed to us that there is such a thing as boreout but have also given it a living and tangible face, namely their own.

Introduction

The world of work in the 21st century: from burnout to boreout

Workplace stress is simply part of today's world of work. It seems as though anyone who is not stressed is not important. For this reason, the problem is often exaggerated. Of course, there are genuinely stressed employees who are being squeezed like lemons by their companies. But there are also those who experience the opposite. That is what this book is about. Statements about stress should be taken with a pinch of salt: not only does stress sound important, but it is also socially desirable – and has a substantially higher conversational value than boredom, for example.

The topic of stress at work dominates many conversations at parties. And yet, if the talk goes any deeper than superficial banter, it suddenly becomes apparent that many employees are actually far from being stressed. On the contrary, they

are understretched, unmotivated and immeasurably bored
– with no hint of a challenge or any interest in what they do
at work each day. According to a survey by Kelly Services,
an international employment agency, the overall European
average for employees who feel stressed stands at 27 per
cent.

Of interest to us in this book are the remaining 73 per cent
– all those employees who place themselves somewhere
between 'stress level just right' and 'understretched'. So, it's
not about stress, but rather about the opposite: it's not about
burnout, but about boreout.

Being understretched, unmotivated and bored in the world
of work in the 21st century? Now, you probably think this
is utterly impossible in this age of globalization. We should
be overstretched rather than understretched. Who, exactly, is
bored at work? But just picture for a minute your professional
environment: do none of your work colleagues leave you
wondering exactly what they do all day? What their tasks
actually are? Who perhaps even give the impression of being
stressed, but who aren't working under stressful conditions?

It's worth considering the results of a couple of surveys:

- A poll by the Gallup organization indicates that in
  Germany, 87 per cent of all workers feel only slightly if
  at all committed to their companies. The study suggests,
  among other findings, that as many as 7 out of 10 of those
  questioned do not feel they have a job that really suits
  them.

- In 2005, Dan Malachowski interviewed more than
  10,000 employees about the topic of time-wasting in the
  workplace for Salary.com and AOL. The result: 33.2 per
  cent of this group declared that they did not have enough
  to do at work; in other words, they are understretched.

Thus, despite all that we hear on the subject, countless employees are under no kind of stress; rather, they actually have 'free time' at work. And the amount of this free time is not as little as you might think. To cite the investigation by Salary.com and AOL once more, the poll shows that the understretched employees spend two hours of every working day on their private affairs – things that have nothing to do with work and for which they are actually paid. They write countless private e-mails, surf the internet for their own amusement, and use the enormous number of websites to help them fill the time they are at work. Then there are websites with games, in which you can score points for races with office chairs, or get tips for passing the time in boring meetings, or brand new videos explaining how you can make a fountain out of a cola bottle and a packet of peppermint sweets. Some bored employees even develop their own business ideas and plan how they will free themselves from their current workplace. It is surely evident that not all of this comes under the category of 'creative breaks in the working day'.

There are software firms that can calculate with pinpoint accuracy how much time can be saved with faster programs or computers. The time lost due to slow hardware and software is equivalent to two workers per year out of every 500. Yet here we're only talking about a few seconds per employee per day. That is a minuscule amount when compared with the time that many people simply do not work and yet sit in the office. There, every day, hours are being wasted because staff are not applying themselves to their actual work.

Salary.com and AOL have calculated that this phenomenon costs the United States over $750 billion dollars a year; that is over $5,000 per employee. According to the Gallup study, estimates of the total economic loss in Germany run to over €250 billion. Even if the figures are slightly high, a sense of being understretched, unmotivated and bored is obviously, despite globalization, very widespread in the working world of the 21st century – and its effects impose considerable costs.

Because many unsatisfied employees prefer to deal with private matters in the workplace, rather than attempting to overcome their feelings of dissatisfaction, one might be tempted to say it's their fault and to write them off as essentially lazy. However, we should guard against that. The surveys about dissatisfaction we have cited also reveal that although those understretched employees are the most dissatisfied, they actually wish that they could be more active. So they have either ended up in the wrong career, or it is the companies themselves that are preventing these employees from taking on more challenges.

The dissatisfied employee adopts various strategies in order to appear busy and keep additional work at arm's length. This behaviour is a paradox because these strategies themselves intensify the condition of dissatisfaction. Employees adopt them because they assume it is more enjoyable to do little or next to nothing at work. But the truth is different: a long period of doing next to nothing at work amounts to endless and horrifying tedium. Merely pretending to be busy becomes wearisome with time and, above all, is unsatisfying. There is no challenge, no recognition. And the employees then take these feelings of dissatisfaction home with them at the end of the day.

When employees are understretched, unmotivated and immeasurably bored, and then actively try – paradoxically – to maintain this condition, they are clearly suffering from boreout.

With the help of the questions shown in Figure 0.1, you can find out whether you or people known to you are affected by boreout. Answer yes or no. Always write yes if you experience the things listed several times a month.

No.	Question	Answer
1.	Do you deal with your personal affairs while at work?	
2.	Do you feel understretched or bored?	
3.	Do you, from time to time, pretend to be working – when you actually have nothing to do?	
4.	Are you tired and jaded in the evening, although you have been under no stress at all?	
5.	Are you rather unhappy with your work?	
6.	Do you lack any sense that your work has real meaning?	
7.	Could you actually work faster than you do?	
8.	Would you rather do something else, but are reluctant to change, because you would earn too little in that job?	
9.	Do you send private e-mails to colleagues during work?	
10.	Does you work not interest you, or have only a little interest?	

Figure 0.1 Indications of boreout at work

If you have answered 'yes' more than four times, then you are suffering from boreout or are on the way there. With this book you can find out what that is and what you can do to combat it.

1

Boreout

Concept, elements and development

The term 'boreout' is composed of two words – 'bore' and 'out'. This combination of words is meant to give the impression of having reached the limit of boredom. Thus an employee affected by boreout is bored out – incapable of being any more bored. Of course, this does not mean that boreout causes an end to boredom, so that change and tension once again dominate. On the contrary, the problem intensifies to such an extent that new, much more serious, consequences emerge for the person affected.

Boreout, as the opposite of burnout, consists of three elements: being understretched, uncommitted and bored in the workplace. Associated with these are long-term strategies of behaviour that the employee adopts in order to appear overloaded and so keep work at arm's length (see Figure 1.1).

Boreout		
Boredom	Being understretched	Lack of motivation
Behavioural strategies		

Figure 1.1   The pattern of boreout

Each of the three elements mentioned has its own character and its own effects:

- Boredom entails listlessness and a condition of help-lessness, because you do not know what you should be doing.

- Being understretched encompasses the feeling that you could do more than is being asked of you.

- Finally, when you have no interest in what you are doing, a lack of identification with your work comes to the fore.

On the other hand, all three elements are always somehow connected to each other and interact with each other. For example, people who are persistently understretched begin to be bored by their work. Those who are constantly bored will sooner or later lose interest in what they do. In this way, the boreout strategies are indispensable, because when people are bored at work, they cannot let everyone see it. How can they allow themselves, for example, to simply sit at their desks and stare into space? That would invite trouble. So they inevitably search for ways of behaving that suggest they are really busy and overloaded. If they do not adopt such behaviour or, more exactly these strategies, they will be in danger of being found out.

Reading this book will lead you into the world of boreout – how it arises and what it looks like. You will be able to relate to the way someone feels when suffering from boreout, and will gain a better understanding of the strategies used to conceal it and their paradoxical character. And, in conclusion, we will present you with solutions that should help you find your way out of the boreout mess, or to negate it.

Boreout is a serious matter. Even so, it is important not to lose your sense of humour in employment, for even boreout has its funny side. So that you don't miss out on this, a fictional gentleman by the name of Alex will accompany you through your reading and tell you a few entertaining stories. Alex has a profound knowledge of boreout. He makes such perfect use of the strategies that he arranges his work routine as he wants and can keep work at arm's length. His superiors do not notice this at all – they are too occupied with themselves. Alex is 31-years-old, works somewhere in the world, in some office or other, and at some desk or other. Alex could surface almost anywhere. There is something of Alex hidden in many of us.

THE RELATIONSHIP OF BOREOUT TO BURNOUT

Although boreout is the opposite of burnout, the two are closely connected. As with brothers, there are many similarities as well as differences. Moreover, brothers – obviously – are related to each other. This is how it is with boreout and burnout: people who suffer from burnout are stressed, have too much work and push themselves to the point of collapse for the company and for their work. On the other hand, for people affected by boreout, the word 'stress' does not exist; they are miles away from having to give something of themselves to their work in any way. Rather, for the most part, they have no idea what it is that they should actually be doing. In these aspects, our two 'brothers' are opposites. What they have in common are many obvious symptoms, which are due to their unsatisfactory situations in the workplace. The connection between the two finally becomes clear when we observe how the two 'brothers' relate to each other in a team, how they mutually influence each other and stand in a Yin and Yang-type of relationship to each other (Figure 1.2).

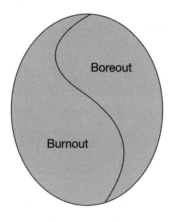

Figure 1.2 Burnout and boreout: Yin and Yang

So, let us treat boreout and burnout as component parts of a system. The system is a team consisting of a boss and his or her colleagues. This team has to get through a specific amount of work. But certain members of the team tend to do more than they really have to, so they take work away from their colleagues. Over time, they give so much of themselves that they begin to suffer from burnout. In turn, their colleagues find that there is less and less work for them to do. They begin to get bored, are understretched and uncommitted. The time they now have free, they use for other, personal things, which, for the moment, they enjoy more: surfing the internet, playing games, making calls, reading a book or even writing – we listed some of the other various diversions in greater detail earlier. The under-achievers begin to suffer from boreout, while at the same time giving the impression that they are permanently busy. Their aim is to keep any extra work at arm's length as much as possible. They enjoy this new free time, at least to begin with – and are falling for the many temptations of idleness. For the most part, the sum adds up: because they seem overloaded, they are given less work. And this same work is taken on by the stressed employees, who become even more stressed in doing so. A self-perpetuating cycle arises, developing its own dynamic through the behaviour of the persons involved.

Figure 1.2 shows these basic interrelations of the distribution of work in a team in the light of both phenomena: burnout and boreout. Here, the behaviour of one influences the behaviour of the other: the stress of those suffering from burnout entails boredom for the boreout group, and vice versa – a relationship in which cause and effect blur into a spiral or vicious circle.

But let's forget burnout for the moment and observe the individual elements of boreout more precisely. We will see exactly what its results are, and how the affected employees experience moments of being understretched, of lack of commitment and of boredom – and what, therefore, is buzzing through their heads all day long.

ELEMENT 1: BEING UNDERSTRETCHED

Employees will be understretched if they feel they could do more at work than is actually the case. Or, put another way, the level of productivity at work demanded by the company does not match the employees' capabilities. Being understretched consists of two elements, one quantitative and one qualitative.

The quantitative element concerns the amount of work. In this case, an employee simply has too little to do; there is too little work or the work available is always distributed to the same people, and the understretched worker is not, or is only partly, one of them. You might be forgiven for imagining that such a thing would not exist in a working world dominated by stress and agglomeration. And yet the survey by Salary. com and AOL, already cited, confirms that the average employee 'fritters away' over two hours per day on surfing or chatting. The surveyed workers were asked why they had so much free time at their disposal in the workplace – and a third of them declared that the reason was that there was not enough work.

The qualitative element concerns the 'what', the content of the work. The understretched employees feel that what they have to do is too simple, or that they are given no real responsibility for designing or creating anything. These people could be doing more for the company, because of the knowledge and abilities they have. The emphasis is on 'could', since the company does not let them do so. Instead, they have to take on the minimally challenging jobs, do the routine work, always the same, while the really exciting activities that involve responsibility land on the desks of other people – often those of the bosses.

How does the understretched employee feel? First and fore-most, unsatisfied. According to the survey by Kelly Services, understretched employees represent the largest group of unsatisfied staff (at 44 per cent); they are, in all, even more dissatisfied than those who say they are stressed. The under-stretched employees feel useless, because they cannot put their abilities to use in the way they want. People who have no chance of distinguishing themselves in the long term, receive no acknowledgement and quickly find themselves being undervalued. Clearly, not everyone has a problem with that. Those who do not want recognition for themselves can quite enjoy being understretched. Others, however, quickly develop a problem if what is expected of them is always too little or inappropriate. For these understretched employees, work quickly ceases to have meaning. A once positive general mental attitude is replaced by an attitude of 'it doesn't matter anyway'.

Alex, for example, always follows the same routine. Day in, day out. The ancient Romans thought that repetition was the mother of learning, but for Alex it is now the mother of his being understretched.

Chewing on a pencil is nothing problematic in itself. Many people chew on their pencils when they are thinking hard. The difference in Alex's case is that he chews his way through packets of them. He doesn't just do it while thinking hard: with him it is a sign of acute understretching.

Alex handles his projects like an assembly line worker. He has just received a new task from his boss: he has to make a cost estimate. His boss is – as always with potential clients – glowing with enthusiasm. Alex, however, sees only the thousandth repetition of the same old thing. 'We don't just make it about the price, but about the quality and the price. Then we are unbeatable!' Alex listens absent-mindedly to his boss, who actually believes that he is combining uniqueness with innovation, and yawns inwardly. Of course, his offers are good and he continually gains new customers, but the trick is fatuous and stale: for the routine jobs, the company hires cheap students, whose salaries are well below those that will appear on the client's bill. The remaining staff positions are cross-subsidized with the money gained this way. How exciting! Alex writes the cost estimate – as always – using the copy/paste method. There is, of course, a big advantage to the company in his being constantly understretched, always performing the same task: he has become extremely efficient at it. But Alex can't stand to look at another cost estimate; he's sick and tired of them. Luckily, there is Sudoku online, so he can do some multi-tasking.

At the same time he continues to chew his way through his pencils. Sometimes he feels that he sees through everything and everyone. He is like a visitor at the zoo: without joining in, he observes the apes – how they swing from branch to branch and chew on a banana with intense concentration. And how they accomplish artificially created tasks that could not be easier from a human point of view.

Alex has begun to incorporate mistakes into his work. On the one hand, it's fun; on the other, it helps him to survive his gloomy work routine. He has delightful fun with his own ideas. Of course, he doesn't want to harm anyone. And yet, it is clear to him that many people simply do not read the documents. That makes building in errors so intriguing. He also has a few ingenious ideas for inclusion in the cost estimate about to be produced: he calls his firm The Chatterers, gives the figures for the project costs in roubles and names his boss the Chief Ape – of course, only in one place: the appendix. But to make things a bit more risky, he introduces a few entertaining details into the main portion of his offer. On a whim, he gives the names of people in his firm to be contacted for information should there be any questions as: for matters of finance, the lady from reception; for checking references, the cook from the canteen; and for international networking, the cleaner. Finally, he invents branches in Togo, Afghanistan and Molvanîa (which, of course, does not exist), and he creates technical expressions that mean nothing: transcognitive tendrakon, semiductive inconstruence and elotaric provincism.

In general, potential clients do not dare to ask questions about these technical matters, and moreover they do not – as we said – look at the cost estimates in quite such detail. What counts is the price, and there Alex has no rival; he is unbeatably cheap – while still ensuring quality, of course. Alex actually does not care. He chews on his pencil, gazes around in boredom and does his job with bravura. He will get these clients too, he is certain of it. And if he doesn't – he doesn't care about that, either. Losing never worries him.

He is looking forward to a day out with his family on the coming Sunday, the highlight that keeps him going through the week. He is going to the zoo to see his children's favourite animals – the apes...

ELEMENT 2: LACK OF COMMITMENT

The second element of boreout is lack of commitment. By this we mean that the employees feel completely dissociated from work and employer. What the employer spends all day doing is irrelevant for these employees; it has no kind of meaning for them. Their actual tasks, the products or areas in which they work, do not interest them and seem utterly unimportant. They no longer care.

This is very different from interested employees, who are alert, eager to know and learn, who care very much about the fate of the business, and who even read the industry magazines and books in their free time. Employees with no sense of commitment never do this, for the topics related to their work do not touch them in the slightest; quite the reverse: the less they are confronted with such things the better.

How do uncommitted employees feel? They see no meaning in work activities and know well how unimportant the tasks appear to them. The topics that fascinate their work colleagues seem alien. If the boss should hand over a supposedly exciting and interesting project to an uncommitted worker, it is with consternation that he or she realizes that the boss really does find it exciting, whereas the poor drone merely dreads having to get involved for hours with something that has no interest. For this reason, the demotivated employee also has trouble with more motivated colleagues. Their excitement and their desire to work seem incomprehensible, and raise helpless questions, such as:

- 'What is supposed to be interesting about that?'

- 'Does it matter to me at all?'

- 'Do I have any influence here?'

- 'How in heaven's name could I possibly think this work was really interesting?'

■   'Why should I have to put myself out for something I don't care about?'

■   'Just who am I doing this for, exactly?'

These workers identify neither with their work nor with the company that employs them. As a result it costs them an incredible amount of effort to carry out tasks that they view as senseless and uninteresting.

The same goes for Claudia, a work colleague of Alex. She too has a job that does not interest her. However, she tries to make the best of it, to Alex's amusement.

Alex has known Claudia for several years now and they work in the same office. They get on well together and trust each other completely. Claudia is responsible for the internet, and she hates her job because it is full of petty things in which she has not the slightest interest, far removed from what she would actually like to do. She has to select news, edit texts and be in regular contact with the specialist departments, who take it out on her every time she has to change the content of her site. She somehow got shoved into this slot after the hundredth reorganization of her company.

Her job does not require her to work at anything like full capacity, so she has a lot of time for herself during the day. And she is using it, too – for what really interests her. During working hours she is developing a business plan for a bar in the middle of the business centre where she works. The name of the bar: 'The Blue Employee'. Her target customers: frustrated colleagues who simply need a drink after a bleak working day, before going home.

When she knows no one is watching, she potters madly over her plan, puts together calculations and thinks about how she would set up the bar. One morning, as she was dreaming her favourite dream, she suddenly realized her boss was standing in front of her. He abruptly fetched her back into the reality of work and unexpectedly asked: 'So, how's the project going?'

Claudia was taken by surprise. 'The bar project?' shot out of her mouth, to which the boss responded in astonishment: 'What bar project?' As she noticed his bemused features, she realized that she had spilled the beans. She could have slapped herself. Alex, who was sitting next to her and was in on her plans, exploded into silent laughter.

'No, ahem,' stuttered Claudia, searching in despair for an excuse, 'I was thinking, we could go drinking with the whole team once a month after work! That's motivating and it promotes cohesion!'

Her boss, a small, plump poison dwarf with a bald patch, nodded quickly, but did not enquire any further. Instead he bluntly informed her: 'You're getting a new project.'

Claudia feared the worst. And, sure enough, the blow then fell: 'You are going to restructure the whole internet site and, together with an agency, write a manual about what our web presence should look like: the firm's logo, fonts, colours, content – the whole package, in fact.'

Claudia almost passed out at the idea of having to discuss such nonsense with some advertising heads. And yet, with some great acting, she replied: 'Great! That's what I call job enrichment! Thanks a lot for this great project!'

Alex couldn't take any more: He gave a snort and ran, feigning a coughing fit, in the direction of the toilets. While Claudia was cursing him inwardly, her boss only shook his head and wondered what kind of oddballs were in his team. 'The project should be finished in a year. Can you manage that?' He was already turning around and scampering off to his next meeting. Claudia shouted after him: 'Of course, boss...' and finished the sentence, mumbling to herself: 'I won't be here in a year's time, anyway.'

Alex came back after a while and sat down again in front of his computer. He too had begun some time ago to think up his own business ideas. Though his A4 notebook started off full of sentences as angry and incoherent as graffiti in a public lavatory, he has made progress since. His current idea: art exhibitions in a disused cemetery. And if that doesn't work, then he'll be a barman in Claudia's bar.

ELEMENT 3: BOREDOM

Linked to boredom is a feeling of emptiness; you have no passion, no occupation. Boredom is generally understood as meaning a feeling of listlessness or of a lack of élan. The employee feels no inner urge to do anything. This is a boredom that cannot be explained, a feeling evoked by nothing in particular. It is just there. However, boredom in the workplace also describes a condition in which someone doesn't know what to do, because there is nothing to do. The work has already been done, by that employee or by someone else. This kind of boredom evokes a feeling of helplessness and even of despair, summarized by the nagging question: 'What, in heaven's name, am I supposed to do now?'

Boredom does not only exist at work. Children begin to get bored if they play with the same toy for too long. Adults get bored because they feel lost in the oversupply of the entertainment industry. And yet at the weekend or after the end of the working day, your time is your own, and you could actually do something to fight the tedium – plan an excursion with the family, meet up with friends, read a book, play sport, go to the cinema or have a snooze.

This is precisely what is denied you at work; there, you cannot do what you want. On the contrary: you know you should be working, since that after all is what you are being paid for, but you just can't – your weaker self won't let you. Every activity requires an enormous amount of effort. And so you begin to turn your attention to things that, for the moment, are more exciting – as Claudia and Alex do. No one can resist the temptation to give in to the inertia of boredom.

When they are bored, employees wait for something exciting to happen. In the meantime, they begin to fidget restlessly, observe colleagues who are working hard and are under stress, while the sufferers from boredom search in despair for something to do. They take refuge in their own internal worlds, think about their next holidays or about what they could do over the weekend, telephone their friends. These activities and others like them are the only ways they have at work to escape from boredom, at least temporarily. In the end, they cannot just go home – they are trapped for the minimum time that their contract dictates they must spend at the office, even if they have nothing to do. And if anyone dares leave his or her desk a little bit earlier than all the others in the evening, critical colleagues will pose the subtly invidious question: 'Are you only working half days now?'

The worst thing about boredom in the workplace is that time simply does not pass. The minutes become hours, the day drags on without end. Insistent questions like 'What am I supposed to do now?' or 'Why can't I just leave?' buzz unceasingly in one's head. That is what it is like for Alex as well.

It is the afternoon in the office. It is quiet; no one really seems to be doing anything. No telephones are ringing. My work colleague Claudia is sitting in front of her computer, her chin resting on her hand, and isn't doing very much except stare at the computer screen. It is nice, after all, to see that you are not completely alone in your boredom and lack of challenge. I have two problems: First: I am bored, I do not have the faintest idea what I am supposed to do. My boss? He's scampering about somewhere in the building. He thinks he is irreplaceable – and so he does everything himself, and I suffer because I simply have too little to do. My second problem: time does not want to pass. I stare at my watch; it is 2.45 pm. I begin to philosophize, plunge into the world of my thoughts. Does a minute sometimes last longer than 60 seconds? Does time deceive us? I cannot imagine it otherwise, for today every minute seems like an hour. The second hand ticks along, tick-tock, regularly, too slow. I pull my sleeve down over my watch and try to get out of time's way. And I am tired, I feel depleted and can hardly keep my eyes open. Microsleep overcomes me, and when I wake I jerk my head up and look around at my colleagues to see if anyone has noticed my little doze. At such times I do the following: I go to the toilet; I sit there, rest my head on my arm and doze for 10 minutes by myself. That helps and, I think, goes unnoticed by anyone. Otherwise I just say I had diarrhoea, and that's the end of the story. I return to my desk. It is 3 pm exactly. I almost feel a physical blow when I think of the hours I have to sit out until I can knock off work. Can I not somehow defy time, get out of its way, to avoid festering with boredom? Perhaps I'll find an interesting article on the internet. I wonder how the employees of 10 or 20 years ago overcame boredom without the internet. A gruesome idea. In the meantime, it is now 3.30, half an hour later than it was 30 minutes ago. That really is something. I go to the toilet again. Thanks be to diarrhoea!

BOREOUT COMPARED WITH LAZINESS

You may be thinking now that we have left out a fundamental element of boreout: laziness. But you would be jumping to the wrong conclusion. Boreout is certainly related to laziness, but not comparable to it in its specifics and its causes. Lazy people will in all probability suffer from boreout, and faster than others. They can properly be called lazy for this reason: because they are work-shy, they have a natural disposition to do as little as possible at work. Moreover, both lazy and boreout-affected people begin to wish for free time for themselves at work, and develop strategies to appear overloaded and keep additional work at arm's length as much as possible. There is, however, a fundamental reason why laziness at work is not the same thing as boreout:

Employees who suffer from boreout are made lazy.

What does that mean? Simply, that there are external circumstances that cause an employee to become lazy or lethargic. Employees affected by boreout are therefore not lazy by nature; they do not necessarily have an inner disposition towards laziness. In due course, we will look more deeply into these external circumstances and the causes of boreout. Let us say this much here: boreout is a complex phenomenon, in which various causes act together. It is not easy to determine which factor is most responsible for people suffering from boreout. It may be that the person affected is basically doing the wrong thing, or working in the wrong place. Laziness is a symptom rather than a cause of boreout. The interplay of various external circumstances pulls people into a boreout-maelstrom and causes them to become lazy. But, as we have already seen, and will examine more closely, the employees themselves contribute to keeping boreout going.

HOW DOES BOREOUT DEVELOP?

Boreout does not announce itself overnight, with drums and trumpets. Rather, the effects of the three elements discussed above must unfold in progression over a long period of time. When they are present to a lesser extent, they can even have positive effects. For example, short periods of being understretched or bored can create space for creativity or improving social contacts within the company; a moderate lack of motivation can lead employees to consider what kind of work would really interest them. Moreover, in any typical working day there are always moments of boredom, understretch or lack of commitment, so all employees experience these symptoms in one way or another at some time in the course of their work, without immediately suffering from boreout. And finally, it takes a while for the affected employee to discover the various strategies of concealment and then subsequently to use them. We can therefore safely assert the following:

- A short chat before the next meeting or a 30-minute slump after lunch do not make for boreout.

- Not every task that is small, repetitive and simple, and that can be quickly accomplished, automatically leads to a condition of chronic understretching.

- Having to do something uninteresting now and then is a part of working life and does not by itself produce a chronic lack of commitment.

The working routine only becomes problematic when the individual elements afflict the employee to excess nearly every day. Then boreout raises its ugly head, and the employee notices that something is not right. This can be seen with the help of Figure 1.3.

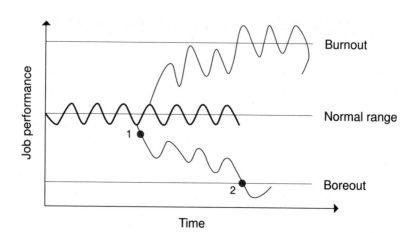

Figure 1.3   Job performance, burnout and boreout

The 'normal' area is that of employees who are basically satisfied with their work, who might occasionally get a bit bored, but for the most part have enough work to do. They are satisfied; their work is challenging and interesting and so is their environment. In short, this is something close to the ideal of a fulfilling working scenario.

From Point 1, employees begin to notice that something is not as it should be: they are seldom challenged, and the moments of boredom pile up. Every day they feel queasy as they travel in to work; the prospect of having to spend the whole day in the office is about as motivating as doing their taxes.

Boreout develops at a creeping pace: the employees begin to use escapist behavioural strategies and to hold work at arm's length, because they are slowly but surely losing their motivation. Such an employee is like a tree that is starting to be eaten away by Dutch elm disease: as yet hardly anything is visible, but the fungus is slowly infesting the tree. At this point, the employee is hardly aware of the change but sinks, unknowingly to begin with, further and further into misery. At Point 2, the tree is dying, and any alert forester would mark it for felling. So it is with employees suffering from boreout – with one considerable difference: they have to solve the problem themselves, while the forester puts the tree out of its misery. By now such employees have come to a point where the ennui has got complete hold of them, and they are unequivocally suffering from boreout: their dissatisfaction is enormous, yet at the same time they have acquired perfect command of the typical behavioural strategies that conceal the problem, thus keeping the condition of dissatisfaction alive.

The temporal progress of a typical boreout career varies from person to person: the symptoms are experienced differently by each individual. While one person may rush headlong into boreout, others experience it as a slower but ongoing process. The intensity of boreout – the extent to which the employee experiences boreout on a daily basis – is also unique to each sufferer.

2

Boreout strategies

Now you know the three elements of boreout. A further integral aspect of boreout are the strategies that conceal the problem, which we will describe in greater detail over the following pages.

Let us summarize: vulnerable employees slide into boreout slowly, not overnight. And yet as soon as they realize that something isn't right, they begin to feel dissatisfied and lose their motivation. They distance themselves from work emotionally; they have no desire to overextend themselves or, indeed, to do much work at all.

The problem, however, is that they cannot openly display this lack of desire to work, because after all they do not want to lose their jobs. For this reason they begin to put on an act of working hard, adopting behavioural strategies that help them to appear busy. These have two aims:

■ to keep additional work at arm's length as much as possible;

■   to gain free time at work to spend on their personal interests.

There are dozens of such strategies, of which we give a few examples here. We are initially concerned with two methods that are simple but well known and effective everywhere: the 'document strategy' and the 'pseudo-commitment strategy'. In the first case, employees sit in front of their computers, surfing the internet and planning their next holiday. Their goal is to appear overworked, so that they have enough time to analyse and compare the various internet offers. Should the boss come by, there are two possibilities: they can close down the screen and pretend to be getting on with paperwork, keeping the printout of some presentation or project on their desk conveniently to hand, so they can write something on it and convey just how busy they are; alternatively they can have the presentation open on the monitor and change the screen view from the holiday destination to the work presentation with one swift keystroke – thus demonstrating why they were looking with such concentration at the screen.

With the pseudo-commitment strategy, you feign identification with the company. This is most simply done by spending more time – albeit pointlessly – at the workplace. If you are the first person there in the morning and almost the last to leave in the evening, you give the impression of having a lot to do. This even impresses those who work longer hours than you do. Either these colleagues are also suffering from boreout and are carrying this strategy to the extreme, or they are victims of burnout and take your presence as proof that you mean business. The pseudo-commitment strategy is very effective, for nothing gives a more negative impression than arriving late in the morning and disappearing early in the evening.

THE COMPROMISE STRATEGY

The compromise strategy (Figure 2.1) entails working hyper-efficiently with full concentration, and not pottering around at a task for hours or even days. The goal is to get a task done as quickly as possible in order to easily beat a deadline set by the boss, who of course is not allowed to know that the work has already been completed. Why? So that the employee has enough time before the actual deadline to turn to personal interests or to be able to chat with work colleagues without being distracted.

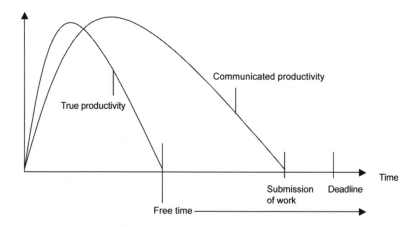

Figure 2.1   The compromise strategy

The compromise strategy has various advantages: should the boss unexpectedly bring the deadline forward, you can present the fruits of your finished work without trouble. Furthermore, you can – if, for example, you are getting bored in the free time you have gained – present the work to your boss a day early, and so depict yourself as thoroughly efficient.

This strategy allows you to control both the other person's level of expectation and your own productivity. And finally, the most important thing to establish: nobody can see the discrepancy between your official and actual workload, so that you achieve your goal of having time for yourself at work, without being found out.

THE LEVELLING-OUT STRATEGY

This strategy, as the name suggests, is based on levelling out the volumes of work. In other words, the work is distributed over a longer period than is actually needed. A long-term project is excellently suited to this strategy. The whole span of time allocated to the task is used, unnecessarily. The levelling out is achieved by pushing the documents back and forth and editing their content in small amounts every couple of hours. Alternatively, they simply lie on the desk for days or weeks without your really bothering with them. Nevertheless, at regular intervals you spend a bit of time on the work, so that you can produce something at any time if necessary and present your results to everyone's satisfaction in the end.

In the meantime, however, you allow yourself little (or rather long) pauses, in which you do whatever you want (see Figure 2.2). In this strategy, too, you convey the impression of being overloaded and having no time for additional tasks. The levelling-out strategy is based on the fact that we have too much time available for the work in hand. Perhaps the employee just has no desire to work quickly, but would much rather potter along slowly, step by step.

This strategy works if the actual level of productivity is always accepted as efficient by the boss or team mates: 'Alex is our most efficient employee: If he needs two weeks for this task, then it just can't be done any quicker!' Then no

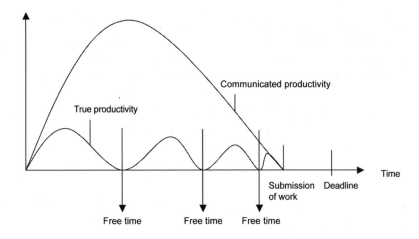

Figure 2.2 The levelling-out strategy

one will doubt that the employee really is overloaded. Once again, then, we are talking about playing a game with other people's levels of expectation. In order for the strategy to be ultimately successful, the result of the work must be delivered punctually and be of the expected quality. The employees can determine for themselves how they spend the greater part of their time up to this point.

STRATEGIC OBSTRUCTION

This is about preventing someone (another worker or a client) from taking measures that would force the employee into immediate action. The aim is not to avoid carrying out the work. Rather, with this strategy, employees manipulate the time at which the work is done, even if this causes possible alterations in the work process and disrupts other people's schedules. Employees may do this if they have to carry out some task that they do not want to do or that just does not interest them. It works in the following way:

Suppose an employee is responsible for liasing with colleagues in order to take forward a project they have in common. But this employee has no interest in the work and would like to postpone it if possible, even if only for a few hours. In order to achieve this, he or she has to find out when their opposite number will be in a meeting or absent for other reasons. (This kind of information can be found in the electronic calendars accessible to everyone in firms.) The employee who, for strategic reasons, would like to delay the start of work, calls up at exactly the time at which the colleague will be absent. Then it is easy to leave a message documenting his or her willingness to work on the project further – without actually having to do it yet. This strategy works because, naturally, no one assumes that anyone would deliberately choose this time to make such a 'futile' call. Yet the employee proceeds according to plan, so creating free time for personal interests. Clearly, the work will have to be done sooner or later, but it is agreeable not to have to do the unavoidable just yet.

Let's have a little quiz at this point: an employee wrote an e-mail to a client on Friday afternoon with a suggestion for a project. At the end of the text he or she actually intended to write: 'I can be reached again from 3 pm today, if you have questions or suggestions for changes.' Shortly before the e-mail was sent, however, that final sentence was deleted and the amended text simply wished the client a pleasant weekend.

Now the question: for what two reasons might the employee delete the sentence? What do you think?

Here is the solution:

■ The client might think it was worth calling to discuss the topic before the weekend. The employee would then have to answer and deal with any questions.

■ The client could have suggestions for changes that the employee would have to implement, or at least line up, immediately – that is, before the weekend.

You have doubtless noticed that the e-mail was quite deliberately sent on a Friday afternoon, since the client is unlikely to want to deal seriously with it so shortly before the weekend. And the employee's goal is achieved: the project and the client do not have to be considered until the following week.

THE BRIEFCASE STRATEGY AND THE HOME–OFFICE LINK

This strategy helps to give the impression that the employee is taking home work that could not be finished during the day because of 'too much stress'. Employees adopting the briefcase strategy mean to give two impressions:

■ That the company is so important to them that they even work in their free time. At the same time, they show that their interest and commitment does not end at the office door, but rather extends all the way home. We'll call this connection the 'home–office link' (HOL).

■ That they are unbelievably overloaded at work and, moreover, that their work is of critical importance, since only important people have to work in the evening.

Here, once again, Alex comes into play. On his way to work he observes the people travelling with him on the train and the bus, especially the well-dressed businessmen. Most of them are reading some newspaper or other, but they never seem to carry it in their hands when they aren't reading it. The secret of the black briefcase is becoming clear:

For years now I've been commuting to work by train. Not because I'm especially environmentally friendly, but rather because it's easier and faster and I can read my newspaper in peace. I felt like an outsider right from the start. I was somehow different from the other passengers; something was missing. It was a briefcase. There are two things I wonder again and again. The first is, what kind of work do these people actually have? They must be important if they carry on working at home after having already spent eight or more hours in the office. As I never bring work home, I sometimes worry about myself: am I doing something wrong? Am I simply not important enough in this world of work? And second, I would be interested to know what they actually carry around with them: secret projects, e-mails and market studies that have been printed off but not yet dealt with? In any case, a load of work is being done at home, it seems to me! I am impressed. There are all kinds of different briefcases, cheap and expensive, brown and black. They all send out the same message: 'I am there for my company even in the evening' or 'Important work does not respect fixed working hours.' Moreover, this importance seems to be a gender-specific phenomenon, since you very seldom see women with such briefcases; but with the best will in the world, I can't imagine that only men could be good managers... In the office, too, I notice that many colleagues come to work with a case, and leave with it too, but I have never managed to catch a glimpse inside. And I can't imagine that Frank, for example, is busy with work for a minute longer than he has to be. One evening when I was on my way home and had to buy something in the supermarket, there was a man with a briefcase standing in front of me at the till. He was paying for a banana, a small loaf and milk. And then, he opened his briefcase. What a disappointment. It was empty! He noticed my glance after he had put his shopping in the case, fiddled awkwardly with his tie, and looked at me as if to say: 'There are usually lots of important files in here.' Then I realized: this is the briefcase strategy, or rather the HOL.

The HOL is becoming a symbol of business, even if sometimes the only things actually carried in briefcases are the day's groceries! The advantage of this strategy is that it is almost impossible to monitor. No one, not even the boss, can ask to see what work his or her 'motivated' workers are taking home. And yet carrying that briefcase doesn't actually mean anything. The main thing is that it looks good and signals devotion to and interest in work, including the sacrifice of free time. Of course, you are living in never-never land if you believe that someone affected by boreout is still working in the evening. The work that accumulates and is left undone is tackled in the office – one day later.

WHEN BOREOUT SECRETLY LEADS MEETINGS

Taking part in a meeting is not actually a boreout strategy as such, since whether you have to be there or not mostly depends on other people. It is possible to adopt the obstruction strategy and delay the inevitable a little, but there is no getting around attending in the end. A meeting is nevertheless a place where you can give in to boreout in complete peace, because there are so many meetings and they last a long time, mostly too long. Boreout artificially prolongs meetings and makes them unproductive, as many people taking part have a 'hidden agenda', a hidden, personal interest. The course of the discussion is determined much more by the participants' boreout than by the aim of bringing the meeting to a successful conclusion.

Our Alex remembers a typical boreout meeting where he had to take the minutes. For him, this was tedious and hardly demanding, but it was fun to observe the participants. He smiles when he explains how the meeting proceeded:

It is 4 pm. The staff members of a medium-sized cooling-unit manufacturer are meeting to discuss the introduction onto the market of a new series of camping refrigerators. The participants include:

- Monica, the leader of the marketing department;
- Stephen, her deputy;
- various other members of the department;
- David, the leader of the communications division;
- Chuan Li, the technician who developed the prototype, connected by telephone conferencing from China.;
- Alex, who is supposed to be taking the minutes.

Monica opens the meeting, 'Good. I am grateful that you were all able to come to this important meeting. I reckon it'll take around two hours.' (General, inward, sighs of relief – people weren't sure that it might not last longer.) Monica goes on, 'We have all received the technical documents from Chuan Li – thank you, Chuan – and already looked at them.' (Monica glances around and sees general, aimless flicking through the documents; David gapes at them openly.) 'First, questions or comments from your side?' (Embarrassed silence, all flick 'interestedly' through the documents with lowered heads.)

David presses the mute button on the telephone and says, 'A bit technical, isn't it, the whole thing? These technicians should be let loose on a customer; then they would realize that no one understands them!' (General smirking.) Chuan Li is switched back on as Monica says 'Super documents, Chuan! Thanks again.'

Stephen remarks 'I have had a look at the market. There are no truly comparable products.' Monica takes up the point, 'So you think we have good prospects for the new line?' Stephen replies, 'I think we do, although the positioning is not yet quite clear to me.' (He then delivers a monologue about how difficult the market environment is at the moment.) 'What do you think, David?'

David, who has been occupied intently with an e-mail from his wife on his PDA, responds with a start, 'Um, yeah, so, I think we should start with a brainstorm.'

(General agreement, followed by silence; no one wants to take the lead as none of them have prepared seriously for the meeting.)

Monica breaks the silence, 'How about if we were to show the whole thing in an exclusive campsite? There's surely that kind of luxury thing somewhere in Cannes, where well-to-do campers meet, isn't there? Just an idea. Our product will be rather expensive, right, Chuan?' (Silence.) 'Chuan, are you there?' Chuan replies, 'Yes, of course, but that's your responsibility, not mine!' David once again presses the mute button, 'Typical, he wants to dodge work again!' (Shaking heads.) Alex thinks, 'As if we are any different...'

David flicks through the documents a bit and suddenly begins to laugh. 'Just have a look at this model. It's the miniature release of the cooling unit that they found a dead body in yesterday. There was a report on the news. Did you see you it?' Stephen grins and retorts 'No, but we could take that on and photograph a corpse in our model. I've already got the caption too, "Keeps your stuff cool" or "Gentle with what you love!"' (Snorts of laughter; David has tears in his eyes and is rolling about laughing.)

As before, the meeting subsides into awkward silence. The competition is discussed briefly, followed by an interlude about upcoming holiday plans, and finally a discussion of just how many bottles of beer the refrigerator would probably hold. Monica disapprovingly asks why it always has to be alcohol. This adds to the general babble about trivial stuff.

Shortly before 6 o'clock Monica looks at her watch, 'Right, I think we have made a good step forward, despite the complex material. (Alex still has no idea at all about what he should put in the minutes.) 'In view of the advanced stage we're at, however, I think it would be best if we were to see each other again in a week's time.' (General relief and agreement.) 'Would that also be OK for you, Chuan?' (Silence.) 'Chuan? Hello? Well, the connection was probably interrupted again.' (Alex considers it much more likely that he got fed up with the senseless blabbering and disconnected himself.) 'Well good, then there's just one other thing: could we now share out the preparation work – first concrete suggestions, timeframe and all that – among ourselves?' (All the participants gulp, clear their throats sheepishly or scratch their heads and remain silent, as if they had heard nothing.)

In view of this reaction, followed by muttered words along the line of 'Stress, no time to do anything more important', Monica gives up. She has to be content with the participants' assurance that they will give it some thought. The meeting is finished; the end of work they had been longing for is finally there.

It would certainly not have been difficult to make this meeting more productive, since the two hours were almost completely wasted. But why should they do that? After all, it is pleasant to talk about non-work topics, to make jokes and laugh. It is entertaining. And there is obviously no time pressure. Far-fetched, do you think? Then go into your next meeting with a pair of boreout glasses on, and you'll see.

THE PSEUDO-BURNOUT STRATEGY AND THE UPROAR STRATEGY

We wish to conclude our list with two further boreout strategies that can help the employee keep work at arm's length or simply appear busy. On the one hand, there is the pseudo-burnout strategy. This is deployed when employees state explicitly that they would fall to pieces under the pressure if they had to take on yet another task. Thus they demonstrate how overloaded they are and so provoke the 'Oh you poor thing' reaction. There may be no truth at all in their claims to be overloaded, but who can prove that? Precisely no one.

Second, there is the uproar strategy. This is adopted when employees have fallen into a daydream, staring for minutes on end at the computer screen without moving a finger or showing any sign of life. When they suddenly realize that they need to look busy, they have two options:

■ to open an e-mail and begin to type haphazardly at the computer keyboard;

■ to take a piece of paper and a thick felt pen that makes a deafening noise, and begin to write or draw meaningless stuff.

Both responses make a racket and make onlookers believe that vigorous work is being done.

These strategies have their funny side, up to a point, but if you can't refrain from smirking on reading this you need to remember that people don't solve their dilemma by using these strategies. On the contrary, the strategies not only cover up the core of the problem, but make matters even worse – as if the dirt swept under the carpet were accumulating in ever-greater amounts. Although boreout victims know this, they still continue on the downward spiral. And that is the paradox, as you will see in the following chapter.

3

The boreout paradox

In order to understand why boreout leads us to behave paradoxically, we can break professional development down into three simple stages, shown in Table 3.1. We will take a closer look at the paradoxical behaviour (Stage 3 in the table) in the next chapter. Here, we analyse three paradoxical types of behaviour, which you no doubt know from your own experience or from your surroundings. Then we discuss the boreout paradox. In this way you will understand why employees suffering from boreout have a conflicting relationship to work and trap themselves in such a vicious cycle of dissatisfaction, idleness and energy-conserving strategic behaviour.

THE 'HANS IN LUCK' PARADOX

In this paradox the elements of wanting and having play the central role; the contradiction is buried in their interplay.

Table 3.1 Boreout and career stages

Stage 1	We are at the outset of our career, with little or no professional experience. We may be highly motivated and are looking forward to professional life and its possibilities. We also know about the dream of sweet idleness, but do not in our wildest dreams think that something like that can happen in real life. We expect stress and a challenge.
Stage 2	We begin work and quickly establish that the world of work is not nearly as stressful as is always claimed. And so we learn to control the amount of work we do, while still sending out the appropriate messages. As we assume that idleness is pleasant, we plan our routines so that we have as little as possible, or even nothing at all, to do.
Stage 3	After some time, we begin to suffer from boreout. Although we recognize that idleness is anything but fun, we maintain this condition. We become dissatisfied and remain so; our behaviour has become self-defeating. We do not try to discuss this with a superior, or seriously consider changing job.

What we have, we don't want; what we want, we don't have. Should that change – should we receive what we wanted but did not have – then we want our previous situation back. One example is relationships. The paradoxical thing about them is that if you have a partner, you may miss your freedom, because you feel constricted. Should you lose such a partner, however, you miss the time together with a loved one and suddenly care less about the freedom to be able to do whatever you want regardless of your partner's wishes.

This to-ing and fro-ing between wanting and having is expressed poignantly in the fairytale of 'Hans in luck'. Hans left his mother and worked for seven years for a rich man.

At the end of that period, the man gave him a lump of gold as big as Hans' head. Hans set off back to his mother, but found the gold was too heavy for him, so he exchanged it for a horse. The horse was too wild for him, so he exchanged it for a cow. The cow was old and stringy, and what was worse, it gave no milk. He exchanged it for a pig. It turned out that the pig was stolen, so he exchanged it for a goose. In the end, he exchanged the goose for a grinding stone that would let him make a new start in life – as a knife-grinder. And in the end he dumped the stone down a well. It was very heavy, and he couldn't be bothered to carry it.

Each time he swapped the old possession for something new, Hans thought himself the happiest person on the earth – but only for as long as it took for a new wish to surface. Whenever he complained and wanted something new, his wish was always fulfilled. Of course, nearly every time he was cheated, but the fact remains Hans had nothing left in the end, and he was happy. The story ends here; we do not know what happens next. Except that Hans returns to his mother with nothing to give her. Later he will wonder to why he threw away the lump of gold through this series of exchanges.

Hans always wanted something other than what he had. That is paradoxical. And normal. Things are much the same for us. As the saying has it, the grass is always greener on the other side. Freely formulated, you could say: we look forward to something that we do not yet have; and when we have it, it will lose most of its attraction. That brings us to a further, similar paradox.

THE GIFT PARADOX

Giving and receiving gifts is often a paradoxical situation, for we do not always get what we want or what really makes us happy. But we have learned to be polite and to thank people nicely. Perhaps we even show enthusiasm and are not quite honest in doing so. 'Do you really like it?' – all of us have been asked this question. The answer has to be a convincing 'Yes', even if we find the tie, book or hand-made candle plain, tasteless and inappropriate. What is paradoxical about this is that we lie for decency's sake. A harmless paradox, perhaps, but one that often arises. If the 'Hans in luck' story was simply a paradoxical situation that dragged on over a long time, then with the gift paradox we are dealing with a pattern of behaviour that is meant – albeit with the best of intentions – to deceive others. Here, our behaviour does not match our feelings. That brings us to the next paradox, where we deceive not only other people, but also ourselves.

THE HEALTH PARADOX

Health is our highest good, and yet we often do things that we know are harmful. We enjoy sweet things to excess and do hardly any exercise. Another damaging vice is smoking. Many people smoke even though they know, and moreover are clearly told on every cigarette packet, that it will damage their health. This too, is paradoxical. In these cases there are cover-up strategies, even from yourself. For example, we may overeat, but compensate by taking only low-calorie drinks. In the same way, someone who starts smoking may ignore the health risks at first. And yet the health risks often become obvious as the years go by; it becomes impossible to avoid the facts. The strategy: you fool yourself and claim that it is not certain that this or that disease actually has anything to do with smoking. Or you simply ignore the possible negative consequences. Only absolutely drastic experiences will bring this cover-up strategy to an end.

AND NOW: THE BOREOUT PARADOX

Let us now end our little object lesson about current, everyday dilemmas and return to the boreout paradox. This book poses the following questions:

■ Why do employees not do something to escape the boreout trap? Why, for example, do they not speak to someone higher up who could help?

■ And why do they resort to boreout strategies that only prolong the condition of dissatisfaction?

Yet it is precisely this behaviour, or rather non-behaviour, that constitutes the paradox. The point of departure of the boreout paradox is...

> ... the great error.

The idea that it is easier to do nothing at work, to trundle along and to have as much time as possible for the things we enjoy – rather like Homer Simpson – is popular.

Employees are often afraid of having to go all out at work. The prospect of too much work or stress drags them down. Surfing the internet, chatting, taking care of personal matters and still earning money – for many, this seems like the ideal occupation. Moreover, there are countless publications suggesting that this condition of idleness is the only realistic option, and far preferable to too much work. We will have more to say about Corinne Maier's discovery of the joy of laziness and the strategies she proposes (arguing that the ideal is to be a passenger, letting others do the work). Scott Adams dedicates a chapter of his book *The Dilbert Principle* to ways of pretending to work while avoiding any effort. In the introduction he promises to reveal his secret methods of doing this, offering the reader a 'ticket to freedom'. The chapter presents strategies for a laid-back life at the employer's expense.

Thus these authors – and others – talk of freedom, offering free time at work as well as satisfaction if the employee adopts such strategies and puts one over on the company. But is it really so desirable to do nothing at work? To have as much unoccupied time as possible and to do anything but work? And even to adopt laborious strategies in order to achieve this goal?

> **We say: no.**

The reality is in fact quite different. For in these moments of boredom, which are much harder to take than a little stress, employees feel dissatisfied and frustrated. And they will inevitably become even more discontented if they adopt concealing strategies. Those are a clear indication that something is not right in the workplace.

We maintain that most employees want to develop and to put their abilities to the test. And they want challenging work that gives them meaning. To get that, they are also willing to put in more effort. Despite all myths to the contrary, then, it is not true that employees wish not to work at work. When they actually manage to avoid doing anything, only then do they realize how bad it feels to suffer from boreout. Then they learn the consequences of keeping work at arm's length. They have to sit out the hours until the end of the working day, and those hours are long. A bit of free time is very welcome, but not too much of it. So employees are far from actually feeling free, satisfied or at in any way happy doing nothing. And, incidentally, the activities they use to fill the work-free time also become boring in the end, to say nothing of the stress of always having to dissemble and to constantly pretend they are working. There, the fun ends and the free time becomes agony.

The foundations on which the boreout paradox rests are as follows:

■ Employees are often afraid of being stressed at work. Inseparably joined to this is the wish to be able to withdraw inside oneself and do nothing in stressful situations.

■ Employees who are doing nothing at work feel anything but satisfied and therefore want to be able to do more work in the moments of boredom.

The paradox is that the employees themselves keep the boreout condition of dissatisfaction alive with the help of the strategies just described, and make no active effort to break out of the vicious cycle.

If you still think, now, that recognizing this problem is unimportant and that the main thing is to have peace at work, then you should think again. It is here that the perfidious character of boreout is revealed: for the strategies are intended to keep others in the dark, to make people believe that the employee is overloaded with work. But the obvious point is that it doesn't work for that person, since no one likes feeling useless over the long term, or spending their whole life doing things that don't interest them. We cannot lie to ourselves. In the end, underworked employees know that they could do more, and know in their heart of hearts that doing nothing does not make them happier, even if they can convince others that they are achieving things.

To end this chapter, let us glance once again at the three paradoxes presented at the beginning, for we did not choose these examples at random. Every paradox shows us a specific aspect of the boreout paradox. With the 'Hans in luck' paradox we made reference to basic feelings and behaviour: that we want things that we do not currently have – the core of the paradox, so to speak. The gift paradox makes reference to the dimension of behaviour. In this situation you know about the paradox, and you behave in a particular way towards the outside world; here lying to others plays a role. In the health paradox we lie to ourselves; we resort, quite simply, to self-deception. All this can also be seen with the boreout paradox:

We want something we do not currently have, develop strategies in order to protect ourselves, and thereby lie not only to others, but also to ourselves.

4

The causes of boreout

FUN FOR EVERYONE?

If you leaf through books dealing with the theory of work and motivation, again and again you will come across the question of whether work should be fun – or even whether fun is permissible at work. Some researchers find that many people just won't do the things that they really find fun. These writers see the solution in re-orientation and listening to the heart. Money, career and status symbols should be valued less highly or even ignored – better poor and happy than rich and miserable. Others believe that a political economy is not able to give everyone work they find fun. There will always be jobs that no one actually wants to do. And they simply have to be done.

The last point is certainly true, but not something that the people who have to do these jobs care about. They do not do the work because some professor postulates that some specific task has to be done from a politico-economic point of view. They do it from economic necessity, or because they simply do not expect work to be meaningful or fun. These people see work as a compulsory activity. We do not mean that negatively, for people can be happy with such an attitude. And in any case – and here we allow that the political economy professors have a point – this work has to be done, and we should be happy that someone does it.

The question therefore has to be understood from individual points of view – for some people it is important to find fun and meaning in their work, for others less so. In view of these two different attitudes to work, we have to consider the question of whether one or the other of the groups could be more susceptible to boreout. Our answer is simple – both are vulnerable. This central piece of knowledge will be useful when we subsequently turn to the causes of boreout.

When we discuss boreout with others, we are told again and again that the only people affected by it are those who believe they have a right to expect whatever they want from their job, and who start to question the meaning of their work. This is not true. In principle, boreout has nothing to do with whether people are looking for a sense of meaning and fun in their job or not.

THE WRONG CAREER CHOICE

All children have career dreams – they want to be firemen, nurses or footballers. They pick their dream job purely on the basis of feeling, for they cannot yet judge what the conditions of employment, career opportunities or earning potential are, or what the day's work really looks like. When they are older and consider their future career in concrete terms, they begin to think over education and job descriptions in their mind. The reasons that affect a career choice can be of decisive importance in identifying causes of boreout. For this is where the first switches are set. When someone decides on a particular career, the chances of boreout occurring are already growing or shrinking.

Have you seen the film *The Incredibles*? It is the story of a superhero family with extra-sensory powers. However, these are precisely the abilities they may not use; instead they have to integrate into everyday work as a 'normal' family – which, of course, backfires. The prime example is Mr Incredible. Horribly bored, he has to handle his clients' insurance cases. And, at least at the beginning of the film, he can no longer do what he actually wants to do, which is to act as a superhero. Many employees today are in the same situation as Mr Incredible: caught in a sense that they have no commitment to what they do or have to do. But why is this so?

People often choose careers very different from the ones they would actually like to follow. They choose the wrong options, and their problems grow from that point onwards. Let us imagine two scenarios:

- Imagine parents who push their daughter to study for a law degree, because they want her to enjoy as broad an education as possible and subsequently have many options. Now, the young woman has a talent for painting and would much prefer to go to an art college, but the parents insist that she can still do this once she has taken a degree.

- A school leaver takes an apprenticeship in a construction company, because the parents think their son should learn something 'respectable'. In so doing, they take responsibility for deciding their son's future, since at the moment he cares for nothing but computer games, parties and having a good time – and has no idea of the seriousness of life. The construction industry not only offers secure employment but is also seen as a worthwhile industrial sector, and the parents expect it will cause the boy to take a more serious attitude to daily life. Besides, young people of this age don't know what might really interest them. They don't really care at this point in time anyway; the main problem is to get them to make any kind of decision at all.

Both decisions could lay the foundations of boreout. The choice of a specific career is often made on the basis of some criterion that seems more important than interest in the work. Examples are (supposed) job security, the prospect of a career, or a higher salary than you could get in the field you would actually like to work in. Do not misunderstand us – we are not arguing for modest incomes and austerity, but we are pleading for a balance: most people need both material and immaterial fulfilment, both money and meaning. This is not an either/or. But people who decide in favour of a degree or a career path that actually does not interest them at all run the risk of sooner or later suffering from boreout.

As suggested above, parents can influence their children's choice of career. There is also pressure from social standards and expectations. If such pressures lead people to choose the wrong course, boredom, under-stretching and lack of commitment are the likely results. And then it becomes more and more difficult to find a way out of the boreout mess. Perhaps our law student will work in a chambers later. And she will suffer from boreout because the law does not interest her and because she finds the work tedious. She would find fulfilment in artistic activity, but she might lack the courage to change; the material penalties would be too great.

THE WRONG LOCATION

Let us vary our scenario and suppose that our lawyer actually did not find studying law quite so boring after all; in fact it was rather interesting at times. But she let herself get seduced into a position in a traditional chambers with formalized relationships and routines, which is the wrong place for her to be. Always the same cases, combined with a dusty, poisonous climate of competition, which makes the work seem senseless to her. Perhaps she would have been happier in a not-for-profit organization; in any case, in this particular chambers she is definitely in the wrong place.

When, exactly, is the workplace the wrong location? Perhaps when the boss takes all the interesting work and only delegates the wrong activities, or none at all. Or when the opportunities for promotion are limited, leading to the employee always having to do the same thing – mostly without seeing the results – and having no prospect of development. Sometimes people just get unlucky when job hunting. The position described sounds very promising, the job hunter is interested by the role that seems to be on offer. But then it becomes apparent that the new work position is sheer horror – the team is boring, the boss does not stretch the employees enough, and the company has complicated and unclear structures. The job hunter actually did everything 'right', really thought about whether the job was also genuinely exciting, but unfortunately all the promises turned out to be illusions.

In short, even the most exciting activity is useless if you perform it in a location that does not suit you. Then, boreout is pre-programmed. Conversely, even if the work location is fantastic and your colleagues excellent company, you will meet with disappointment if you only have material to work with that does not suit you. A great working environment cannot compensate for a lack of interest in the work itself. The wrong thing in the right location will not do.

THE STRATEGIES AGAIN

We now know how boreout can come about: we choose the wrong course from the very beginning, or we find ourselves working in the wrong location. However, there is something we have not yet factored in: the strategies. Remember, intrinsic to the nature of boreout is that we – paradoxically – keep it alive with the strategies described earlier.

With the boreout paradox we have seen that the affected employees seldom discuss the unsatisfactory situation with their bosses. Why do they not do that? At first glance, it seems to be the easiest thing to do. However, that is by no means the case. Instead, employees look for other strategies, clutching at straws that they hopes will save them. There are several reasons for this.

■ when employees first join a company, they are usually still well motivated. They may not have very much to do, but they can see the mountain that the boss takes on daily. Perhaps they approach the boss and offer to take on some of the difficult work. In such cases, however, bosses almost always decline – with some comment along the lines that only they can take care of it, because only they know the details. Or they don't want to take the time to explain the details to their employees. This means that only the boring work is delegated. Once employees have been rebuffed a few times, their reaction is to stop asking and to let the boss bustle about alone, even though they have too little to do, or have tasks that are too boring. The employees are qualitatively and quantitatively understretched.

Now is the time that the strategies come into play. Theoretically, the understretched workers could just do without them and sit obviously bored at their desks, or show their lack of commitment openly at work. It is immediately obvious that that is no use – they would just be handed more boring tasks, things that no one wants to do.

■ The employee fears the (foreseeable) reaction of the boss, who would surely be less than impressed by a display of open boredom. Moreover, many managers take it as an implicit criticism if their employees complain of having too little to do. The strategies are therefore also necessary in order to keep the boss 'off one's back', as is often said, and to avoid a discussion to 'clear the air'.

■ Employees may fear the effort required to change the current situation, unsatisfactory though it is – and with time they find it 'comfortable' to be qualitatively and quantitatively understretched. Here we come to the heart of the matter: the worst thing about a period without work is the prospect of new work. You could change your job, but that means stress and insecurity. You would have to learn something new, and have no desire to do so.

■ At first, we may believe that it is possible to drift through the working day, getting paid a reasonable salary without having to do much for it. Only after a while do we get stuck in boreout and realize that we have drifted into a drab backwater. At this point, however, it will really take a great effort to change this situation. We are stuck right in the middle, and still the tale of sweet idleness moulds our behaviour.

What is happening is that we fear the consequences that would result from doing without the strategies – we have no desire for boring work, but we shrink from an air-clearing discussion or a major change in our working conditions. And, let's admit, all the strategies of deception and covering up are fun – at least to start with. And, when one is worried about maybe losing one's job, it seems much better to keep muddling along and live with the dissatisfaction.

BETTER ALTERNATIVES TO WORK

Continuing to muddle along also seems a reasonable option because there are countless alternatives to actual work in the workplace, alternatives that take our minds off the actual work and make it seem less and less important. The information that can be accessed on the internet becomes more interesting than the boss's drivel, it becomes more and more diverting to send private e-mails through the business net, or to use the unoccupied time to take care of personal affairs.

Think about the work done for sports clubs and amateur drama groups. Have you ever wondered who does all that work? And when does this work get done? We can't suppose that everything is always taken care of at home. Think about journals, internet searches, shipping orders. Certainly, a large part of a club's work is done by people who are not in full-time work. But a much larger part is done by people in work, during work. From a boreout perspective, this is now easier to understand: the club's work is more attractive than the company's. And everything that you bring to it is given for free.

The alternatives on offer in the workplace pull us along in their wake. They take up ever more resources and time, and so become more and more important and exciting. While you are occupied with them it is easy to forget that work is actually boring and that you yourself are dissatisfied. A paradoxical situation: the activities for which, thanks to the boreout strategies, we now have time become the causes of boreout. And they are partially responsible for our staying where we feel do not we really belong. The strategies help us to hide the fact that we are not working, but rather giving ourselves over to all the possible alternatives. In this way we can continue to function without problems – and no one notices. The worst part is that, initially, we do not even notice it ourselves.

DIGITALIZATION DRIVING BOREOUT?

In particular, the digitalization of the office has contributed to our being able to wander everywhere and nowhere. Gone are the days of the good old typewriter, the analogue telephone – and soon the fax machine too. These are all symbols of the old office. The new office is digital: computers with internet connection, voice-over IP telephony and e-mail are already standard. In theory the employees become more efficient, the paths of communication become shorter. That is what is interesting about the company. If you look at these tools through a pair of boreout glasses, however, you see the whole story somewhat differently.

For these tools also make possible many alternatives to doing any actual work, and provide further ways to waste time. Take, for example, the internet with its giant world of information and diversion. Newspapers can be read online, exotic travel destinations can be searched for; you can even read a book online. Especially exciting and popular are games of all kinds: card games, running and jumping games, games of mental exercise and many others. The links for these can be sent all over the world via e-mail. Alex, too, indulges in this passion and, in truth, he is not the only one in his office.

Alex has just received an e-mail, one of around 20 or 30 that land in his inbox every day. Most of them are of a private nature, as this one is. His friend Hugo has sent him the link to an online game. Alex often plays such games, and Hugo knows this. Today there is a game by the name of 'Hit the Penguin'. The aim of the game is to hit a penguin from behind with a club so hard that it flies through the air as far as possible. Alex likes that. At first he felt guilty about playing games at work. He even considered forwarding the e-mails to his private inbox so that he could play them at home. This burst of morality was, however, short-lived. 'Why should I play at home, if I have enough time for it in the office?' His colleagues have also applied this line of reasoning. So he forwards Hugo's link to them. Within minutes there is raucous excitement throughout the office. The whole team is playing and leaving work to one side; there are even bets on who will send the poor penguin the furthest. A giant jamboree. Alex enjoys this quasi-strike. Such incidents are common, and everyone openly recognizes them, simply because everyone is doing it. Normally, everyone plays a little by themselves, inconspicuously but frequently. Alex still makes an effort to appear busy while playing, so that no one cottons on. But there are colleagues who are already completely indifferent to appearances. Although anyone could look directly at the computer screen, they play on unconcerned. Sometimes the company puts a line through the account and blocks certain websites – usually those with the games that have spread throughout the company. 'Laughable', Alex thinks. 'As if these control measures could stop me playing.' And with that, he pulls out his mobile phone and disappears into the break room.

Alex therefore feels in good company, and is not alone in his firm. For this reason a significant marketing industry has already evolved, built on the boredom of employees, or rather on their need not only to work at work but also to fill up the free time there. We are talking about viral marketing. An advertisement spreads via the internet and e-mail, in the same way as a virus. The recipients are millions of bored employees all over world who mostly play or look at games or adverts during working hours rather than at home. Typically, e-mails are sent with a link to an internet site where you can win something (a coffee machine or a car perhaps) by taking part in a game. A company running its marketing in this way finds a form of advertising that is exciting for its potential customers, while the employees suffering from boreout can relieve the tedium of the workplace with a game.

And finally, let us not forget the mobile phone. It lets employees phone or write an SMS whenever they choose. Thus they no longer need rely on the communication tools that the company has put at their disposal. The mobile telephone provides a constant source of diversion.

NORMAL, BUT BAD

Now you are probably saying that some of these things are quite normal. And here we actually agree with you. What is so insidious about the whole thing is precisely that the causes come on so 'normally'. Wrong choice of degree, wrong choice of job, absence of challenge, personal internet connection: all quite normal. As we said, boreout does not announce itself with drums and trumpets. The causes are everyday stories. Boreout does not need a scandal, a catastrophe or a ruined career. On the contrary, often everything goes well, all according to plan. Only when all the elements are combined, only when conditions become utterly unsatisfactory in themselves and for the sufferer does boreout arise. And that, too, is quite normal, for here you will also know of countless examples, from your own surroundings, that appear to you totally mundane. Everything is normal – but nevertheless bad. And fatal in its consequences. That is why the diagnosis of boreout is so important, as only when it is recognized does it become possible to make changes – and make things better.

5

The symptoms of boreout

In this chapter we want to follow up the question of how boreout expresses itself in affected persons. In doing so, we need to draw a distinction between the way the sufferers feel in themselves and the way they behave at work. Let us first venture to tackle the latter and have a look at how an employee suffering from boreout behaves in the workplace.

CAN BOREOUT BE OBSERVED FROM THE OUTSIDE?

You may have sometimes wondered what exactly your work colleagues actually do, and what they are busy with all day. If you know about boreout, certain patterns of behaviour take on a different meaning: the bustling activity of your neighbour is suddenly revealed as nothing more than a helpless attempt to hide gaping boredom. The symptoms make it possible to unmask a person suffering from boreout. Of course, we don't want to call for targeted and systematic testing, for when managers start to analyse how long their workers spend on the internet or how many e-mails they are sending, then trust is called into question – which could make it harder to deal with the possible work-related causes of boreout. Do not test, but rather observe.

If someone is aware of the existence of boreout, then, the concealing strategies can be seen through and behaviour in the workplace suddenly shows another face, one that, despite all the unhappiness, is in many ways amusing. Our Alex has begun to observe his colleague Erica as she 'works'. And he thereby discovers an interesting pattern of behaviour, which is related to four important locations in the office.

Actually, at first glance everything looks normal. Erica is not overloaded right now, admittedly, yet there is apparently no obvious sign that she is suffering from boreout. Not yet. But here is the straw that broke the camel's back: she has moved. She has changed her desk – not her employer. She now sits at the edge of the room with her back to the window, no longer in the thick of things. What does that have to do with boreout? A great deal.

I have been watching Erica for three months now. She used to sit roughly in the middle of our open-plan office, separated off by glass partitions. She attracted my attention for the first time because she looked so busy, and yet was often to be found outside in front of the entrance, smoking or talking on her mobile. Then I began to trace her strategic pattern of movement, and came to a surprising conclusion – she lives by the 'four-location principle'. Desk, coffee corner, entrance area and toilet. Something was clearly not right: the time she spent away from her desk was simply too long. So I began to watch her more closely, and soon diagnosed a case of intensive boreout.

The course of Erica's day seems to be roughly as follows: she arrives somewhat later than most of us, and then leaves somewhat earlier in the evening. She takes a leisurely lunch break, but then eats a small salad at 2 pm in front of the computer at her desk, which gives the impression that she is dedicated and under a lot of stress. In reality, she is mealtime-outsourcing so as to have more time to shop and take care of personal matters during her actual lunch break. The impression she makes has two advantages: she appears busy and indicates that she only has time for a snack. That is healthy, but also a cry for help, for release.

Erica often goes to the toilet. This is not bladder weakness, nor a sign of acute, long-term diarrhoea; I do the same when I need a nap. Erica can hide in perfect peace in the toilet. There, she does not have to put on an act for the outside world, but she can simply sit there and 'be'. The toilet is the last refuge of stressed boreout patients. The key to achieving nirvana – the WC door, which can legitimately be locked.

Erica has a mobile phone. That is practical, as with it she can call from anywhere, even outside the office. She does this often. We know the disadvantages of open-plan offices: private telephoning is hardly possible, so people try to dodge their way outside, as Erica does several times a day. Even there, she feels the pressure of time: she cannot telephone in such a way that it looks like a private call. She must pretend calls are business-related. Remember the little number with the salad: the pressure of time leads this boreout patient along step by step. If she is aware of the problem, she can skilfully manipulate the signs. Giving a private conversation the appearance of a business call, with appropriate facial expression and supporting gestures, is one of the most difficult tasks. Of course, she also has a reason for always going outside: she needs a cigarette break. This too helps her to send out a signal: namely, that she combines her smoking break with a business phone call and so wastes less work time. Bit by bit, however, Erica has become more careless, and so I begin to see through her camouflage.

After a short – very short – detour to her new work desk she often slips off to the secretaries; it seems a good place for a chat. Erica has begun to use the internet to exchange photo albums, to discuss hotels and shopping opportunities, and is found more and more often chatting with the secretaries. She seems to have fewer and fewer inhibitions about putting her boreout openly on show. And yet again and again there are cute little attempts to hide the lack of work, the boredom: for example, while Erica has an impressive file, clearly relevant to work, open on her computer screen, she has minimized this and is flicking through a couple of women's magazines on her desk. The message is clear: a lot to do, but taking some time out in the interim for a moment of relaxation. But that message has nothing to do with the reality. That was and is the other way around: not much document, a lot of magazine.

Erica seems to be comfortable with her new work desk. Here, she is less subject to the pressure of observation, as only the tree outside her window has a free view of her computer screen. Now she can do business on the internet, pick holiday destinations, can pile up women's magazines on her desk – and she still has the options of the secretaries' area, the coffee corner and the toilet. The four-location principle is still her guide. And the pressure to put on an act has been lessened, at least in one location.

So, if the sufferer has such a command of the behavioural strategies that no one really notices the lack of interest, the boredom and the sluggish pace of work, then of course there are no clear symptoms. Only if you are fully aware that workers could be suffering from boreout do you recognize the patterns of behaviour that could reveal it. The symptoms that can be noticed from outside provide your first evidence. Of course, evidence is not proof. However, when the signs multiply, and when patterns emerge from them that correspond to the strategies, then it is reasonable to conclude that they are symptoms of boreout.

The external symptoms are less unequivocal than the internal ones: while it is initially possible to lie to yourself, once you have read this book you will not be able to fool yourself any longer. Assessment of boreout is a matter of honesty, the diagnosis of the syndrome in others – and admittedly also about voyeurism.

One thing that happens quite often in the workplace can reveal cases of boreout very clearly – only if you already know about it, of course, but you do know after reading the story of Erica. We are talking about moving your office location – an often laborious business that has its good and bad sides. You know: once every two years you change your desk, floor, building. You only change your location, not your job. So you move with colleagues, most of whom you have known for a while. Now, you have to agree about who should sit where. This can give rise to a lot of discussion, and with it we are at the crux of the matter. There are often good and bad positions people can choose. So which are the bad seats – and which the good? You will often hear: 'But it's much louder over here!' or 'The room seems darker and bleaker over here!' There is also the: 'This is a bad seat to have, because you sit with your back to the door.' That seems plausible, and anyone who has heard of Feng Shui knows that the general harmony is disturbed when your back is to the door. Further arguments are put forward: 'If I'm sitting with my back to this glass partition, anyone can see what's on my computer screen. That's not smart, especially when clients come over.' Well noticed. Of course, this is actually an argument against anyone sitting there at all. Or do some workers have more important data than others? Hardly. For here we are not dealing with keeping secrets or Feng Shui. We are dealing with just one thing: with boreout and its strategies. When the department is moved to a new location, you will quickly notice who is fostering these. Most of those affected by boreout do not want other people to be able to look at their computer screen without any warning, so they are not the least bit thrilled to be sitting with their back to the door, to a glass partition or to the aisle without having an office plant or a rack to reduce the view.

They will use all sorts of excuses: health, peace and quiet, the need for confidentiality or even Feng Shui – Feng Shui is very popular – but if you watch your colleagues after a move you will quickly find that they are often pretending to be busier than they really are. And that at some time or other they get to have a wall or a plastic tree behind them, for walls may have ears, but no eyes…

WHEN PEOPLE SUFFER INWARDLY FROM BOREOUT

Returning to Erica, whose work patterns we described earlier, she seems at first glance to have succeeded very well in freeing up time at work. And yet we know that appearances are deceptive. In fact she will not be able to put up with this state of affairs for long – if she honestly admits to herself that she is dissatisfied with her situation. Over the long term she is actually wasting a lot of energy on her cover-up manoeuvres. But in the short term, too, she would have to put in a lot of effort if she wanted to change things. For this reason it will take a long time before she admits to herself that she is ill with boreout, and actually instigates changes. What interests us in this connection is how she actually comes to the realization that she is suffering from boreout. Inner symptoms weigh disproportionately heavily compared with the outward signs that Alex has noticed. For here we are dealing with the consequences of boreout for the whole person, with the emotional state that accompanies the sufferer all day – not only during working hours or during their free time at work, but also in their real free time outside the workplace.

For this reason, in this section we will also use the term 'affected person', or just 'sufferers', since after work is over they are no longer employees, and yet are still affected by boreout, or rather its symptoms.

Let us begin with the morning of a typical workday, heralded by the ever-familiar sound of the alarm clock. Anyone who suffers from boreout or is on the way there will sense a queasy feeling in the stomach shortly after waking up. It is a feeling of unhealthiness, triggered by the prospect of spending the whole day at work. It is not that the sufferers are sick to the stomach. But they think about what has to be done at the office, what will confront them during the day. They think about the problems and tasks, meaningless and always the same, and about how little they care about all that. They curse the monotony that has them in its grip: always the same train to work, always the same fellow-passengers; always the same workplace, always the same people; and in particular a job that does not motivate them in the slightest, and whose most exciting times are long gone. This feeling peaks with the sigh: 'How tedious it is to have to go to work again today!'

That is how the sufferers feel as they go to work. How they feel once there we already know: miserable, helpless, bored of course, uncommitted, understretched. On top of that they feel they have to dissimulate, which is often stressful and tiring. They suffer as they struggle with dissatisfaction and frustration. When they are at work, they experience boreout most intensively, since in the end it is exactly this work that makes them feel so bad. They adopt the strategies and keep the tedious things at arm's length as much as possible. With time, it can get to the stage that even genuinely exciting activities no longer interest them, and they protect themselves from them with the strategies as well. In this way, they count their days as wasted, and only the prospect of the evening after work or of the weekend (which is too short anyway) brings short moments of satisfaction.

It is after the day's work is over, however, that boreout shows its truly invidious character. Invidious because the symptoms of dissatisfaction can no longer be so easily attributed to boreout, and because it cannot be simply switched off at the touch of a button when the affected person leaves the office. At the early stages, sufferers may not yet realize that their malaise in the evening could be related to work. So, after close of business they go home. And although they have not done much work all day, although they are now free from work and can do whatever they want, persons affected by boreout tend to feel 'under the weather'. This is expressed in various ways, as outlined below.

Tiredness

Sufferers feel tired, lackadaisical and depleted. They feel lazy and, for lack of energy, give in to this laziness. Let us make the point again: laziness is not a cause of boreout, but much more a consequence of it. The affected person only wants peace and falls asleep in front of the television.

Irritability

The sufferers easily get irritable, as they have brought the sense of dissatisfaction home from work. They feel sullen and overreact to every little thing. Their partners can suffer from their spiteful behaviour while having no idea of the true emotional state of the sufferer.

Listlessness

The affected person has no desire to do anything, although he or she has already spent the whole day doing not much at all. After work or at the weekend would be the time to engage in encouraging hobbies. To start with, these help in blotting out the frustration pent up during the day. However, with time, the divide between free time and working time becomes blurred – and there is no sense of fulfilment in either sphere any more, because of boreout.

Introversion

If sufferers are naturally somewhat introverted, then they increasingly lock themselves away from the world. They are imprisoned in their dissatisfaction and bottle up the negative experiences of the day. If parents or friends bring them back to reality with the question: 'And? How are things at work?', they answer cagily: 'Well, everything's OK, got a lot to do, as always!' And so they begin to construct a façade.

To conclude this section, let us briefly turn our eyes in a different direction and once again observe the fraternal relationship between boreout and burnout. The symptoms – much more than the causes – show similarities between the two phenomena. For the symptoms described above can also be observed in burnout, as can a feeling of inner emptiness, of uncertainty or even despair about whether one will ever find a way out of the dilemma.

However, some specific symptoms are primarily found in people affected by burnout, bringing the differences once more into the foreground. That can help us to better understand boreout, in that we can define the borders between it and burnout:

■ People affected by burnout often devote much of their free time to work-related matters; those affected by boreout, in contrast, have no interest in anything to do with their job. They don't waste a second outside working hours on worrying about the company's problems.

■ Those affected by burnout feel overloaded by work, while with boreout, the sufferers are confronted by the opposite: they are understretched, feel not the slightest challenge. The person affected by burnout is stressed, while the person affected by boreout only acts that way.

■ Burnout sufferers feel 'drained'; people affected by bore-out feel 'bored'. For them, time drags on in an unbearable eternity of emptiness. A moderate degree of boredom is not so hard to cope with – it seems long certainly, but one can conceive that it will pass. But if boredom simply carries on and on without end, then at some time or other, you are simply going to be bored out. Then you have reached a different level of misery.

In conclusion, boreout shows itself both during working hours and in free time. What can be observed of boreout from the outside is evidence of the problem – but only visible if you are aware of the phenomenon. The inwardly discernible symptoms are mostly suppressed to start with until, with time, the sufferer notices that something is not right. The invidious character of boreout leads to the affected person also feeling dissatisfied outside work, and then the malaise spreads to the home as well. Signs of underlying depression show themselves. Of course, there are employees who can draw a sharp distinction between work and free time, and who simply forget about how they've felt all day at work. Most people, however, are about as successful at this as they are at simply leaving private problems behind at the entrance to their office. As soon as boreout also becomes obvious outside the workplace, then the time has definitely come to start thinking seriously about the work routine.

AND THE CLIENTS?

We have described how boreout displays itself with affected employees. So far, though, we have not tackled an interesting question: are the clients of a company also indirectly affected by boreout? Given the abundance of bored and under-challenged employees, a client will inevitably at some time or other come across one who is dissatisfied with his or her work and so no longer provides full services for the client.

Although every – yes every – company believes it has perfected the art of customer satisfaction and first-rate customer service, there are many instances of poor performance. Have you as a consumer been treated badly in the past? There are countless examples:

■ You would like to book a holiday and are sent the relevant information – but a full week later than agreed.

■ You would like to renew your third-party liability insurance, but have to wait for weeks on end for an appointment.

■ A complaint that you have made is not taken seriously.

■ You are dissatisfied with something and threaten to take your custom elsewhere in the future. The answer: 'Yeah, of course you have to decide that for yourself' or merely an indifferent 'And?'

We can all recall such depressing experiences. That answers the question we asked earlier: yes, boreout can definitely influence a client's consumer experience. Here, we are not dealing with the question of which strategies the employee can deploy to avoid work. This time, we are setting the focus much more on the dissatisfaction that results from boreout, which clients will quickly become aware of. Boreout can certainly express itself through poor customer service. An employee who suffers it is not interested in the client's requests or problems. This is not surprising, as boreout is not easy to avoid. It costs the sufferer an enormous amount of effort just to get the work done. As much effort as, for example, it costs you if you have to invite a distant, slightly unpleasant acquaintance to dinner when you have absolutely no desire to do so. You resolve to call him or her, but put it off day after day because you dread making the call. Finally, you do the inevitable and pick up the telephone. So it is for employees suffering from boreout who have to discuss matters that seem utterly uninteresting – even intensely boring – with clients they do not care about.

So, the next time you come across an unmotivated employee, consider whether perhaps boreout could have had a hand in it. Or, conversely, ask yourself whether the client that you are currently talking to on the telephone has exposed you, or rather your boreout.

6

Who is affected – and who isn't?

When looking at the causes of boreout, we must turn our attention to the individual factors. Why does someone suffer from boreout? After reading this book, you will know whether you are affected or not – if you are completely honest with yourself.

We want to turn to more basic considerations. To this end, we will increasingly look to the environment and the structures in which boreout can flourish. On the one hand, we want to demonstrate that practically all employees can be affected by boreout, but we also want to highlight the more improbable or near-impossible cases.

WHAT PROTECTS AGAINST BOREOUT – HIERARCHY OR POSSESSION?

A simple statement to begin with: those affected by boreout are employees who work for a company that does not belong to them. For the most part, such companies are constructed hierarchically: there are the employees without particular responsibility (the majority) and the bosses who are involved in the actual running of the company (the minority). In general, you would expect the majority to suffer from boreout and the minority from burnout. Accordingly, a position high in the company hierarchy seems to be synonymous with a greater sense of involvement. But that is not always the case. For people's relationship with work and with the company results not from the position they hold but rather from their personal connections to the firm. A senior position in the hierarchy therefore does not inevitably protect against boreout; even those with responsibility can suffer from it.

Alex is beginning to think carefully about the phenomenon of boreout and wants to know whether it can also be found among senior managers. He gets in contact with some of them, pretending to be a journalist who wants to research the problem – but without success. The executives are silent on the topic of boreout. For this reason, Alex has imagined how an interview with a CEO might go:

Alex: How are you today?
CEO: Excellent, many thanks for asking. Every day in the office is a joy and a challenge!

What he actually means is: 'Well yeah, I'd feel better if I were on my yacht somewhere in the Mediterranean.'

Alex: Thank you for taking a short time out all the same. I hope I haven't interrupted you during something important?

CEO: Oh no, don't worry about it. I am, of course, mightily stressed, but, as a man in an important position [leans back in his leather chair and seems to be thinking: 'God, am I important?'], I know that you have to face questions from the public every now and again.

What he actually means is: 'Do you have to come now, just before 4 pm? Because I wanted to go and play golf today!'

Alex: Are you proud of your career?

CEO: I am, by nature, a modest person, who has always worked hard for everything. It is less about me than about the task that I have to accomplish in this world, in particular in my company. There is simply no time left for singing one's own praises.

What he actually means is: 'Clearly! All the bunglers from my school years haven't got nearly as far as I have! And I can honestly say to myself: "I was just always in the right place at the right time and have somehow never got myself into hot water."'

Alex: Was your whole life marked by hard work?

CEO: When I was young I realized that you have to put some effort in to get what you want. I have held on to this motto all my life since.

What he actually means is: 'They were so mean to me in school and always picked on me, saying: "Look, the swot with the specs! Are you going back home to mummy? Ha, ha!" So I took refuge in books and studied.' (He is crying inside.)

Alex: Have you ever been bored at work at all? Or felt understretched?

> CEO: No! Whatever are you thinking of! Boredom is an
> alien concept for me. And all my jobs have always
> presented an interesting challenge!
>
> What he actually means is: 'Well, back when I had my first
> individual office, once I simply had to lock the door and
> have a nap on the floor. My job was simply too boring,
> always the same; I just couldn't take any more!'
>
> Alex: Can you understand how it is that some employees
> in your company are suffering from boreout?
> CEO: I have read about this phenomenon, but I can
> assure you of one thing: it does not exist in my
> company. We are like a large family, get on well
> and talk openly about everything. Moreover, the
> jobs we offer are exciting. And do not forget: we
> have a well-trained management, who take the
> worries of our workers seriously.
>
> What he actually means is: 'Ah, you know what? As long
> as my salary arrives on time and the company doesn't go
> bankrupt because of this boreout thingy, I actually don't
> care.'
>
> (The conversation ends and the CEO disappears off to the
> golf course.)

The case depicted here is hardly an exaggeration. The material rewards are high at the top of companies, and that creates distance. Moreover, employees in senior positions often have their own offices and those lower down the scale know little of what goes on there.

The more isolated the top managers appear and the harder it is to understand what they actually do, the more probable it is that they are doing nothing at all. The CEO in our interview certainly has critical things to be concerned with – but he also meanders through the day, in the same way as some of his under-challenged junior staff. Even in the executive suite, then, the level of stress can be exaggerated. There is still enough time for many things other than work.

Alex's fictional interviewee is interested in golf, like so many people in management positions, among the men at least. And so it makes sense for him to give his golfing magazine the attention it deserves, or to combine a business meeting with a client with round of golf. Who would imagine that he might take this burden on himself for anything other than purely business purposes? Who would suspect that the pseudo-networking strategy helps him to stay away from work for longer than is necessary? No one. But is it really necessary to have so many distractions, so often?

Let us turn the screw and put the question differently: would CEOs or senior managers act in the same way if they were working for their own company? Hardly. For then, they would feel guilty about frittering their time away on trivialities. And here we have identified a decisive factor: ownership in a business. People in charge of their own businesses put heart and soul into their work, and certainly do not suffer from boreout. For they are intensely involved in what they do. They make heavy demands of themselves, and there is no way that they would adopt the strategies we have described. That would be like saying: 'I am now going to practise the uproar strategy – just to see if I notice that I'm actually not working at all!' It is therefore inaccurate to say that all workers are susceptible to boreout – not everyone suffers in that way. For example, freelance workers are very unlikely to be affected, since their sense of involvement is almost always high. Being near the top of the hierarchy does not protect against boreout, but ownership of the company does, as does working for yourself.

And, of course, the 'normal' employees, the majority, may also show enthusiasm for work and demonstrate the will to rise up in the company ranks. But there's the rub: the company often prevents employees from becoming more involved; instead it leaves them working in isolation, understretched, unmotivated and bored out.

A further structural element of hierarchical work relation-ships is the opportunity for business trips. Those near the top of the hierarchy have more scope for such travel. The ques-tions here are obvious: Who gets to go on these trips? How often? And why? And the opportunities are not distributed equally and can lead to injustices. From a boreout point of view, a business trip can be a good opportunity to break out of the grey routine of work or to feel one is not endlessly con-fined to the office. This means that two parties are affected: the one going on the trip and the one left behind. And both will experience and live through boreout in their own, special way. Let us first listen to a more senior employee, the 'one leaving', before we turn to a more junior member of the department, the 'one left behind'.

The one leaving

I feel pretty good. A couple of days in Rome isn't bad, after all. This is the fourth time our corporate group has sent me over to Italy. The meetings are not really essential, but I do find it's good to make personal contact. And Marco, the local project leader, is a good colleague of mine. Of course, I have arranged the meetings so as to have a bit of free time too. Thursday from 10 am is ideal – there is time set aside to relax a bit; then I've arranged to stay Friday as well by arranging a meeting at midday over lunch, and on Saturday I have time to go shopping. It's a good feeling to know that I have to fly over to Rome because no one there can sort things out as well as I can. And anyway, I won't need that many meetings to clarify the outstanding questions. When I'm back in the office again at the start of the week, no one will be asking exactly what I've been up to. So I can completely book up Monday and Tuesday in my diary for finishing off the work from the Rome visit. And yesterday, on Wednesday, I was in preparation meetings all day.

Taken altogether, with the two meetings in Rome, it makes a whole working week away from the office routine. Of course, I don't much care what comes out of it in terms of solid results. The important thing is getting the wording right on the report. I need to lay out the stages of the project carefully and make clear that a follow-up will soon be necessary. Next time I will arrange a meeting on Monday at 2 pm in Rome. That'll mean it's not worth going into the office on Monday morning and, as the meeting could go on for a while, I will get on the return flight on Tuesday. I'll get the evening flight – by then all the other flights will be fully booked (who will ever check that?). Then while I'm there I may be able to arrange a business dinner on Tuesday evening, so that I'll have to put the flight off until Wednesday (or rather my secretary will). And given what might happen then (perhaps I'll have to meet someone else on Wednesday morning) I reckon I'll finally fly back on Wednesday evening. And there you are: another couple of days in Rome on my schedule. The important thing is to make sure the team back home have plenty of work to do, otherwise they'll get bored. And start asking questions.

Of course, from the assistant's perspective such a business trip looks somewhat different. When the cat's away the mouse will play; the assistant sees everything from the point of view of someone who has been left behind and is suffering from boreout.

The one left behind

While the boss is off abroad, the team is stuck here in the building. And so am I. I wonder why the boss has to travel so often. And why I am never allowed to go on these trips.

I have a theory: the boss goes on business trips because no one else can do what's needed over there. That goes for me, too. The daily routine changes when the boss is away: You can get on as well with each other as you like, but the boss is still the boss. When there's no one watching what we're doing, we seem to behave differently – more like we actually are. It goes like this:

- I come in to work a bit later. [Note: that only works if the team culture allows it and no one squeals to the boss about lateness.]
- We take a few more breaks during the day, and they tend to last a bit longer.
- After lunch I treat myself to a second espresso and do not rush straight back to the office.
- As I arrived at work a bit later in the morning, I make up for it by leaving a bit earlier in the evening. That is, so long as I'm not expecting a call from the boss to check up on me – if I am, I must remember to divert calls to my mobile.
- I can finally surf the internet freely, without constantly having to call up ready-made Excel tables on the screen to hide what I'm doing. It is wonderful: for a while at least, I can do without my strategies.

STAFF RESPONSIBILITY FOR BOREOUT

As regards boreout, an especially interesting role is played by the personnel or human resources (HR) department. It has the task of ensuring that everything runs smoothly in the company and that all employees are generally motivated. So HR should not be affected by boreout. We want to dig deeper and cast light on the relationship between HR and boreout.

Boreout should actually be a thorn in the side of HR. What do you think: does the HR department suffer from boreout? We can find a suggestive clue in a saying that is common among HR managers: 'Even the employees' unproductive time is in fact productive (so-called "creative waste"), as it gives scope for interpersonal relationships, the company culture and people's own well-being.' Could this statement indicate that they have resigned themselves to the bad (the 'waste') and, by using the word 'creative', prefer to stress the positive than to see what's staring them in the face?

Let's take an analogy: suppose a mother suffers from klepto-mania and teaches her children that, although stealing is not actually right, in certain situations it is quite acceptable. That's how it is with the personnel department. HR managers who suffer from boreout will preach zeal for work to their colleagues, but then every so often they will gladly arrange so-called 'teambuilding occasions', which mostly achieve nothing except to provide an escape from work and hence some relief from boreout. Boreout is bad, of course, and is not to be tolerated, but sometimes, just sometimes, it should be overlooked. As with the analogy of the kleptomaniac mother, the HR bosses do everything possible to avoid being discovered themselves, to divert suspicion onto others and – as with teambuilding activities for example – to create opportunities for living out the 'addiction' together. This can be legitimized in superbly ingenious ways: 'Yes, the event was somewhat long, expensive and laborious – but it was fun.' Of course it was: in the end no one had to work.

This is not a sweeping attack on teambuilding and the HR bosses. But it is clear that not everything is being done to pre-empt boreout. The personnel department is not immune to the malaise, even though keeping track of such issues is actually one of the core competencies of this department. Put it another way: even police can suffer from kleptomania.

BOREOUT INTENSIFIED BY DESK JOBS

Now we want to look into the issue of which sectors are most prone to boreout. In the main, it is a phenomenon of our service economy and the professions developing within it, where people work – mostly at desks – basically by themselves and can present woolly results. It arises in professions where people are under stress during peak periods, but for the greater part of their time do not know what they are supposed to be doing, other than reading magazines or surfing the internet.

And then they face a dilemma, because it is exactly this kind of behaviour that cannot be openly indulged in.

In Switzerland they call a task that you have to do at some point in the future, but that you know about in advance, an 'open issue'. Now, there are professions where there are no 'open issues', to-do lists or tasks that can be completed later. A bus driver drives a bus and does the job then and there. Similarly, those who work in the cleaning industry, who do their work and when they knock off must leave everything clean behind them, have no open issues. A clerk or office worker, however, typically has many different upcoming tasks. As office workers also work relatively independently, they can decide the tempo at which they manage these open issues, and thus can easily fall back upon pseudo-burnout strategies. People with such jobs can control their work processes relatively independently.

When you have no desire to work and are under no pressure to carry out upcoming tasks, you can simply push them further into the future, or pass them on to someone else within the team, ideally without the recipient's noticing. Open issues and tasks that can be disposed of relatively freely can therefore quite definitely be seen as boreout catalysts. That is why desk jobs are more vulnerable to boreout. And where workers can decide for themselves when they will carry out their tasks, that is an important factor in the onset the boreout strategies – it makes it possible to put these strategies to use on a broad basis.

JOBS LESS LIABLE TO BOREOUT

Do you think waiters often suffer from boreout? Some can, for example, act as if they haven't seen you when you want to pay, and just sit placidly behind the counter reading a newspaper. There are the ones who bring you the menu at the beginning of the meal, then do not surface again for the next 15 minutes, while you have no idea where they are. Perhaps, behind the apparent refusal to take any notice of the customers that we have surely all experienced in restaurants, there is hidden boreout?

Boreout among taxi driver seems less likely. They can hardly pretend that they are always carrying passengers, and leave the people waving at them standing on the pavement. It is just as unlikely that police officers will watch a burglar or a drug-dealer without doing anything, because they don't want to have to type up a report. Here, we are dealing with jobs where work has to be done at a particular moment and the workers must respond immediately and do what they are employed to do. Clearly, they can attend to this with more or less motivation, the work may fail to interest them, can bore them or understretch them. But unlike people in the desk jobs discussed earlier, these workers can't simply pretend to be doing their jobs like actors in a pantomime.

In some professions or situations, boreout is in fact extremely rare. For example, could nursery carers suffer from boreout? No, that is hardly possible, because they cannot adopt strategies that help them just pretend to be attending to the children. They have enormous responsibilities and have to be constantly alert. Or what about surgeons? Could they be tempted, during an operation, to use some kind of strategy to avoid doing the work properly? Again, they cannot because they too carry enormous responsibility. If they forgot that (which is what the strategies lead to), it would have the direst consequences.

Alex has considered how such an operation would proceed and how a surgeon suffering from boreout would behave (a situation that, fortunately, only takes place in Alex's head and so belongs in the realm of fantasy):

In the operating theatre Mark (the surgeon), two young assistant doctors (Maria and Adrian), a theatre nurse and the anaesthetist have gathered together. A patient lies on the operating table. He has to have a leg amputated. Mark suffers from boreout. The operation begins.

'Doctor, shall we proceed as usual?' asks Adrian. Mark gives a start, 'I just have to clean the scalpel, you go ahead.' Maria, slightly puzzled, answers 'OK, but please come back quickly.'

Mark goes off to the side and begins scraping away at his scalpel. He squints with one eye at the operating team, while with the other he observes the gleaming blade and rubs it with a cloth.

Adrian becomes impatient, 'Doctor, you should really come now.' Mark looks for a new excuse, 'Hang on a second, my rubber glove is pinching. I'm just going to get a new one.' He rummages around in a drawer, pretending to search for another glove – knowing full well that that there are no gloves in it. In the meantime, the operation has already begun.

Maria looks impatiently at her boss. Mark notices this and can no longer delay. He comes back to the operating table and glances helplessly at the point to be operated on. 'A difficult case.' He skilfully ignores their bewildered glances and starts a new attempt at not having to do anything,

'Something's just occurred to me: have we tested the blood compatibility?' He glances expectantly around, studiously ignoring the anaesthetist, who is actually responsible for this. Blank faces. Maria glances back and forth around the team and finally asks 'Why should we do that?' Mark replies, seriously and calmly, 'You can never be too careful. I'll have a quick look at the dossier. You can carry on, of course, it will probably match up after all, but just for safety's sake...' The anaesthetist seethes with inward rage.

Adrian and Maria glance at each other, feeling worried, while Mark makes himself scarce. He goes out of the room and runs down the corridor. Both doctors rack their brains figuring out what they should do now. Mark goes to the secretaries and asks for information, 'Could you please check the patient's blood group once again? While you do that, I have to pop into Room 214 for a visit.'

The secretaries set about their task, while Mark hurries up to the next floor and locks himself in the toilet. After 10 minutes he returns to the secretaries' desk, gets the details and hurries back towards the operating theatre – however, he does not enter the room, but hides behind a plastic tree, as the two assistant doctors are now coming out. The operation has obviously been interrupted. 'Just where has the boss got to?' Maria asks. 'Hopefully that stuff about the blood group is right, but I still don't see why he suddenly wants to check it. Let's just wait for a while.'

Mark is still standing behind the plastic tree and observes the two doctors from a safe distance. After three minutes, they disappear in the direction of the secretaries' desk – he grabs his chance and runs into the operating theatre, where the rest of the team is waiting. 'Everything's OK', he says. 'But now where are our two colleagues?' 'Looking for you' is the reply. Then Maria and Adrian come back and ask Mark where he has been. He answers, 'I have established that everything is OK. But now I see that the pulse is very weak. I reckon we ought to postpone the operation.' Adrian gapes at him in disbelief, 'But why?' Mark murmurs something to himself. The rest of the team is astounded, but they keep their feelings to themselves. Mark has years of experience, after all, and he is the boss.

What you don't know is that tomorrow Mark will either have another appointment and not be able to do the operation – or he will quite simply be ill, for surgery is among the most difficult of activities when you want to hide boreout symptoms.

Since we looked at the service sector in detail earlier on, now we want to briefly consider two other sectors of our world of work: agriculture and industry. Let us begin with the former.

Boreout cannot arise in agriculture. Or do you know of farmers who do not milk the cows because they simply can't be bothered? Because they are bored by doing the same thing morning after morning? Or who believe no foxes would ever harm their hens, and so leave them outside?

Inconceivable! Of course, they can be bored or find their work uninteresting. Farmers can even be lazy, but they cannot adopt deception strategies and simply pretend to do the work. They have to carry out the necessary tasks whenever they arise.

We find the same when we turn to industry. Machines must be operated, cars assembled and checked, or walls for a house put up. In industry, a concrete result is necessary – something visible, measurable outcomes. That makes it difficult merely to pretend. Assembly line workers are engaged in repetitive activities that are subject to strict testing and equally strict measurement. Companies call these workers 'shop floor people'. For the most part, they earn less than the company average, operate within narrowly defined time limits (often having to clock on and clock off) and their results are measurable. Here boreout, and particularly the adoption of boreout strategies, would quickly lead to dismissal. It is, of course, conceivable (and even probable) that assembly line workers are unmotivated, understretched and bored. They may even be lazy, in individual cases. But they do not suffer from boreout as such. Because what counts here, too, is that there are no strategies for avoiding it.

Workers in agriculture and industry do not suffer from boreout because measurable results are demanded and the boreout strategies will not work. Perhaps this is why 'honest work' is often talked about in these sectors: jobs in which you have to deliver, not blather.

INDUSTRIALIZATION AND SPECIALIZATION: TWO DEVELOPMENTS WITH CONSEQUENCES

A short, abridged excursion into the history of work should cast more light on the origins of boreout. The precondition for its development over decades was created at the end of the eighteenth and the beginning of the nineteenth centuries, with industrialization.

For, with that, work became a product, and there emerged the new basic principle of 'securing a livelihood': people no longer worked primarily for themselves, but rather for someone else. The employer paid a wage, so that people could, among other things, buy those items they had previously grown or made for themselves. In this way, work became gainful employment. The philosopher and theorist Karl Marx was already talking about alienation from work in the middle of the nineteenth century: according to his theory, factory workers are alienated from the product, because they can neither gain an overview of the process of production nor be in any way involved with the final product. The workers, according to Marx, have neither a legal share in the product nor a right of co-determination nor a continuing interest in the company as a whole. You do not have to be a fan of Marx – as we ourselves are not – but no one seriously doubts that alienation is a result of industrialization and can have negative effects on interest in work in itself. Alienation is significant when you look more closely at the emergence of boreout.

Closely associated with this new kind of work – gainful employment – are the division of labour and thus specialization, as well as the emergence of the company. Employees now have to make a conscious choice of a specific activity in a company, which in most cases does not belong to them. In the pre-industrial age this choice was made for them, or rather the question was never even posed: people worked directly for themselves and their families. Gainful work and hence the division of labour have led to specialization. From this arose three connected problems:

Too many job models have emerged. Even a few decades ago, the spectrum of possible working activities was relatively manageable. Most were in agriculture and in industry. This changed with the rise of the service sector. In the course of globalization new business models arose, and are still arising almost daily. The division of labour became ever finer; an increasingly complex economy evolved, with previously unknown jobs.

At the same time, the scope of work in any particular job became increasingly narrow; people had to specialize. Add to this the fact that no individual can now gain a broad overview of the myriad activities offered on the job market. Owing to this extreme division of labour, the individual stands in danger of not finding exactly the kind of work he or she is genuinely interested in. It is becoming increasingly difficult to find the right thing; or, to put it another way, the probability of not doing what you are genuinely interested in is strongly increased by the division of labour and specialization. Two factors deserve particular notice:

■ There is little opportunity for a change of occupation. Specialization makes it increasingly difficult to change between different kinds of work: the hurdles are mostly too high for a move to another profession or another company. If you have spent years acquiring the special skills required for a specific position, then you are not so well qualified for other jobs that do not require precisely this expertise. Specialization obstructs access to other occupations that would, perhaps, interest you more. You therefore get trapped in the work you know. It is all the more important, then, to decide on the right and not the wrong course from the very beginning.

■ Workers are distanced from the product. The fact that people no longer work for themselves, but rather for a company, creates distance from the product. What Marx called alienated work means, in concrete terms, that in many cases employees have no identifiable relationship between their work and the end product. In particular, the company where they work is often anonymous, huge, international and impersonal – alien, in fact. Of course, there are exceptions, both on the part of the company and on that of the employee: even large companies can create a personal climate, and not all employees have a problem with anonymity in the firm. Nevertheless, a product that is irrelevant for the employee is the ideal breeding ground for absolute lack of commitment at work.

7

The different phases of boreout

Many people think that a little boreout is no boreout at all. Muddling along a little every day, working on one's own, having free time for personal matters, getting on with things as they are and accepting the lack of challenge and the latent dissatisfaction simply as givens, as facts of life – that sounds quite good, actually. It is like a chronic illness, where you get used to the symptoms over time and they come to seem quite normal. Consequently, many people are convinced that their case is not one of 'real' boreout. The syndrome is found only in a few particular cases – they arise only now and again and have no real importance. But when we look a little closer, some interesting points emerge:

- Boreout is not equally bad for (or part of the expectations of) everyone.

- Not everyone talks about their lack of productivity when they first become aware of it. People may simply suppress

the problems, or assume that everyone feels the same
about work

■   The various problems related to boreout are actually not
as negligible as they appear at first.

So is a little boreout no boreout at all? Far from it. For there
is the road to boreout and there is imprisonment in boreout.
On the one hand, then, a 'little' boreout can get worse – once
again, like an illness, which may either worsen or get better.
Boreout can exist in a mild form and develop dangerously –
and can most easily be cured in the early stages. But you can
also be 'ill', suffering from boreout, for a long time. And this
suffering, too, exists at various levels – more or less intensely.
Not everyone is equally understretched or unmotivated. Not
everyone is underachieving to the same degree, or spends the
same amount of time on their personal interests. So you can
suffer more or less from boreout – it differs in each individual
situation.

And be on your guard: the fact that you ostensibly make the
best of your unsatisfying situation does not mean that you
are not suffering from boreout – even if you suffer rather less
than other people.

FIVE TYPOLOGIES

On the one hand a diagnosis is something very individual.
On the other, the boreout phenomenon as a whole can also
be generalized: there is a kind of clinical picture, rather as
there is for 'flu. It is something individual, but nevertheless
there are certain elements that always occur. And there are
nuances that make 'flu 'flu.

We have given plenty of clues for individual appraisal on the
previous pages. In this chapter we would like to set out five

typologies, which show in general terms what boreout can look like. We hope this will help prevent imminent boreout being overlooked in cases where only minor symptoms can be observed. This kind of judgement helps in recognizing small indicators, assigning importance to them and counteracting them. Of course, we don't want to make a mountain out of a molehill: we accept that molehills are molehills, and only wish to point out that you can still trip over them. And that, under certain circumstances, these particular molehills can sometimes turn into mountains.

The five typologies are, however, not only provided so that you can get a sharper focus on your own situation and recognize the first signs of boreout. They are also intended to give boreout a face. And they should make it possible for you to classify colleagues suffering from boreout, to conduct a first analysis. The typologies, as we have set them up, increase the chance of recognition, and the clinical picture takes on more solid contours. In naming the types of boreout we have joined various elements together: causes, symptoms and individual characteristics. This also naturally includes the kind of people who are untroubled by boreout, and it is with them that we begin.

The Samaritan

Samaritans flourish in their vocations. They implicitly understand the meaning in their work, and get enjoyment from it. They help where they can, and their work is directly integrated into their lives. They have a balanced private life, and their work flows into this in a good way. They do not get stressed by work, and are well able to take care of their families and to develop friendships. They do well financially, but are motivated by the work itself. They are self-aware and satisfied with their jobs. These people do not suffer from boreout.

The journeyman

The journeyman wants to learn. These are workers at the beginning of a path that can develop in many directions. However, there is already a slight, dark shadow over their daily routine. Not everything fascinates them, not everything is a learning experience. They are motivated and look forward to the day when they will be assigned an important role, but here and there signs of a certain boredom – a sense that the work offers too few challenges – are creeping in. The journeyman workers put up with these moments of doubt, seeing them as inevitable discomforts on the upwards road. Moreover, they are well paid and have good prospects of promotion to higher things. On the other hand, they definitely see advantages in not always being stretched to the limit, and use a bit of spare time now and then for a few personal affairs. These people are suffering from a mild form of boreout.

The *Titanic* passenger

We all know what happened to the great liner. The passengers naturally suspected nothing to begin with, just like our *Titanic* passengers. When the journey began, there were no signs of impending doom; only once it had struck the iceberg did it become clear to everyone that the ship was anything but unsinkable. The daily routine of the employees we will call *Titanic* passengers is comparable to the complacent routine on board. They have mastered the strategies for concealing boreout very well, but cannot yet admit to themselves that the free time won through those strategies has its downsides. They still believe in the fairytale of the lotus-eaters; they are in effect halfway to boreout. They often work on boring projects, they hear company news without much interest. They could actually contribute much more towards the success of the department – but they don't; instead they skilfully paint the poor work they do as something much greater than it is.

This is a middling level of boreout, and the iceberg is coming into sight.

The chameleon

The chameleon can adapt to its environment. This is important for an animal, and is pretty much the only thing most of us know about the chameleon under normal circumstances. The strategy of adapting to its environment in order to live is, so to speak, the animal's core competence. So it is with the daily work routine of the chameleon workers: they have a superb command of deception strategies. There is no situation in the workplace to which they could not adapt in order to avoid doing anything, or to put work off. They completely control people's perception of their activities – in particular, the boss's. Chameleons are understretched, bored and unmotivated, look after countless personal matters in the course of the day and take far too long for everything they do. No one notices: the strategies work perfectly. If their managers asked the chameleons at short notice to explain what they do on a daily basis, that would surely be the greatest challenge of all. These workers are suffering intensely from boreout.

The maggot

A typical maggot eats its way through meat, which obviously is better off without it. From the outside the maggot's work cannot be seen; the damage only becomes apparent when the meat is cut open. The maggot is a classic parasite, and maggot employees are the horror of every company. They epitomize the ones who contribute absolutely nothing. They turn up at the office punctually enough, but leave behind no visible signs of 'work'. When they are away on holiday, nobody notices. The maggots never need to delegate their tasks during their absence, because there is nothing to take over. They make not the slightest contribution to the smooth running of the business – quite the reverse. If the maggot were to leave the company, people would see absolutely no change in the progress of work. The consequences would only be felt in the accounts department – positively. While chameleons every now and then produce something positive and show what they are capable of, this element is entirely lacking in the maggot. Despite all this, the maggot somehow manages to stay in place and may somehow even acquire an aura of importance. The maggot is the undisputed boreout king. A higher degree of boreout is not possible.

To avoid becoming a maggot, and find ways to start fighting the boreout before it is too late, it is important to find a solution. At this point, however, we would first like to warn you about falling into the trap of pseudo-solutions! We will discuss this further in the next chapter.

8

Pseudo-solutions do not help

In the past few years, row upon row of books offering pseudo-solutions have been published, with titles along the lines of *The Elephant Strategy: How you can steamroller everything in the office to your advantage* or *The Lemon Principle: Don't let yourself get squeezed dry*. These works are entertaining and can be read simply for light amusement, but at the same time they claim to offer the perfect solution to all the problems of the workplace – although the claim is not always entirely true. They give you tips about how best to handle intolerable situations at work, how to present yourself in a better light (without really having to do anything) or how to get promotion without actually being qualified for it. These tips are typically passed on in terms such as: 'Always let your secretary take your calls, never fill the photocopier with paper and make sure your job title appears on all your e-mails. That increases your value.'

Some books of pseudo-solutions turn out to be particularly successful; they are discussed and taken seriously, because many people really believe they will improve their careers by following the advice the authors offer. In these books, laziness is no longer treated as a problem, but rather proposed as a solution: laziness as a way of putting one over on the mean-spirited company.

LAZINESS IS NO ANSWER

We have already emphasized that laziness is not the cause of boreout. Employees suffering from boreout are not lazy per se; rather they are made lazy. But as laziness is closely related to boreout, we want to deal with these pseudo-solutions in greater detail. We are dealing with the question of whether employees are best off if they disguise their idleness at work and bury all their hopes for satisfaction and success.

The French author Corinne Maier has recently released a book with the title *Hello Laziness*. However, the word 'laziness' plays a central role only in the title and right at the end of the book. The work itself is, rather, a sweeping attack – a settling of accounts with the capitalist system, the large companies and indeed with nearly everything that has anything to do with them. Education? Does nothing. Information and communications technologies? Useless. Motivation at work? God forbid! Ms Maier's credo is: learn the art of doing as little as possible or, best of all, nothing at all at work.

Certain aspects of the book are extremely interesting and offer points of contact with boreout. The author draws attention, for example, to the nebulous talk of corporate culture, which has made it impossible to identify and measure success. There she has really hit the mark, because boreout incubates in a climate of goals and methods that cannot be measured. The woollier the goals, the more it festers. Meetings are also insidious, according to Corinne Maier: she seems them as pointless, serving only to 'overload' managers and put them under stress that they would otherwise not suffer. What is also interesting is her conclusion that most people are over-qualified for their position – in a boreout sense, this means unmotivated, understretched and bored. At the end of her presentation, the author looks at strategic approaches that allow employees to look busy, and presents her 10 counter-recommendations for not living up to the company's expect-ations: she advises working as little as possible, never under any circumstances taking on a post of responsibility or choosing the superfluous posts that exist in the largest companies, and above all, avoiding change.

Maier thus describes how an employee can, in her opinion, avoid all the unpleasantness bound up with work. Her approach is targeted at ensuring that nobody should ever give in to illusions about work – such as, for example, the illusion of challenge or success in the workplace, or of being able to achieve something in the company.

If such illusions are still swirling around in their heads, em-ployees should bid them farewell. Maier's solution, explicitly stated, is to surrender to fate and react to the oppression of the company with irreversible subjective withdrawal and discrete but merciless parasitism – thus becoming the maggot, the failure of the company.

It is our firm conviction that this approach is neither practical nor desirable. It totally misjudges reality – both the reality of the world of work and also, more importantly, the world of human feeling. We have established how employees really feel when they are bored, understretched and unmotivated. If they feel useless or have constantly to work at things that do not interest them, they feel miserable. They become dissatisfied and frustrated. Corinne Maier's advice, however, leads straight to this condition – it is badly thought out, and is, in fact, a recipe for boreout. What are people supposed to do all day, then, when they have found an 'undemanding little position'? Pick their nose? We maintain that nobody likes to be seen as a failure, and yet, according to the author, this is supposed to be the goal. In suggesting this, she does not solve the problems (which certainly exist!) of the employee in the workplace, but rather exacerbates them. Moreover, it is an illusion to think that you can give in to the laziness at work that she extols. Of course, by the use of disguising strategies the employee can create free time and so achieve the state of idleness she advocates. But, sooner or later, such behaviour ends in bitter dissatisfaction.

Our tip:
Be lazy at home instead and reject these and other pseudo-solutions. You spend enough time at work without trying to seek idleness there as well. As you surely already know, we are certainly not saying that the world of work is easy or that everything always runs like clockwork for everyone. View it rather as a challenge and do not give in to fatalism.

CHECKS FOR BOREOUT?

Not only the employees themselves but also companies can be tempted to seek a pseudo-solution to the boreout phenomenon. One such error is to adopt the pseudo-solution of checking up on employee behaviour.

Various kinds of checks can be imagined. On the one hand, there are checks on the IT equipment that many employees use to pursue their personal interests: checks on the number or even the content of private e-mails, or more precisely on the internet behaviour of individual employees; checks on telephone records and fax dispatches, as well as the documents produced on the printer that have nothing to do with work. On the other hand, companies could also keep watch on social behaviour in the workplace: not only the length and duration of coffee breaks, but also, for example, the ways employees plan to meet external deadlines or whether they have specific strategies in place for systematically keeping work at arm's length.

Some of these measures are already being taken today; the appropriate technical means exist in droves. The company can use them to reduce to range of 'alternatives on offer' that employees can choose rather than getting on with real work. But these efforts meet with only moderate success, as the example in Table 8.1 shows.

Table 8.1 A pseudo-solution and its consequences

The aim:	The company wishes to prevent employees from sending free SMS messages over the internet.
The measures taken:	It blocks the free web connection, so that employees cannot send SMS over the network.
The employees' response:	The employees sneaks their mobile phones out of their bags and send their SMS that way.
The end result:	The employees are still sending SMS despite the blocked internet sites. Painstakingly writing out the message on the mobile telephone takes much more time than if they had typed it on the computer.

As you can see, the company can always reduce the number of alternatives on offer, but that achieves nothing. It can check up on the employees, but that too is fruitless, because the company has not solved the problem, but just tinkered with the symptoms. And what will the employees do? Perhaps come up with even more ingenious strategies for getting around these checks as well. If it adopts such an approach, the company will end up with inspectors who themselves are suffering from boreout or, if the checks lead to summary dismissals, have to endure drawn-out court proceedings. The approach does not work, since all it tries to do is tackle the symptoms. It simply assumes that the employees are not behaving properly, without asking why. And the worst thing is that, if the inspectors do not properly understand what is going on, their misconceptions may muddy the waters further. A lasting solution to the problem of boreout must therefore begin with its roots. The affected employees themselves need to recognize, for example, that they are actually injuring themselves. Managers, for their part, need to devote the time they are spending on checks to looking at the affected employees and confronting them. In particular, the managers should take a good look in the mirror and ask themselves why their workers are behaving in such ways.

Checks and denunciations do not lead to a motivating work climate where reliability, efficiency, creativity and, not least, fun and trust can thrive. They offer only a pseudo-solution that does not make any lasting impact on boreout. Such approaches should be avoided.

9

Individual responsibility as an instrument against boreout

Before we look in detail at our proposals for solving the problem, we would like to clarify something: the responsibility for boreout must be shared among many people. There may also be many who could contribute something towards its elimination. But there is only one person who can truly solve the problem. That is you, yourself. 'We are all the architects of our own fortune,' as a wise old proverb has it. This means that we need to take control of our own lives before asking what others can do for us.

The notion of individual responsibility assumes that individuals are the ones best placed to take their destiny in their own hands and to take responsibility for themselves and their decisions. But in the daily office routine, which is largely defined by the work contract and the tasks imposed from above, is it really possible to speak of individual responsibility? Yes, it is. Because for all the restrictions that are imposed on you at work, it is up to you to deal with the work you have and the (sometimes limited) freedoms available on the company's terms. The developments in workplace design of the past 20 years are clearly going in that direction: open channels of communication, mobility and inclusion in decision making are the component parts of the 'new' ideologies in terms of the theory. In concrete – practical – terms, this means that employees are expected to approach their tasks actively, develop new ideas without being asked, be in a position to determine their pace of work, and manage their jobs according to what is best for the company. An understanding of individual responsibility has become a basic requirement in many job descriptions. No one now wants grey office workers who just mechanically complete the work set before them. 'Entrepreneurship' – business mentality – is the slogan, and generally without ifs and buts.

Individual responsibility is appreciated by those who do business. Individual responsibility leads to individual initiative; without it, people would just do a task without actually following it up. It is when problems arise – which is indisputably the case with boreout – that it becomes clear why, in such a situation, individual responsibility plays a key role and why it is the individual employee who must act. It is the individuals who know the reasons for their dissatisfaction, and who must look for ways to change the situation. Neither their mothers, nor their work colleagues nor the boss can do it for them. Of course, there are cases when the sheer pressure of having to work in some particular place prevents employees from recognizing their own responsibility – because they simply cannot manage to find another job, because they have no alternatives or because they fear reprisals from the company if they dare to speak openly of their problems. For exactly this reason, we want to explicitly point out the responsibility of the company. A company has a duty to treat its employees well and to help those who cannot, or can only partially, appreciate their individual responsibilities. It is up to the company to create structures so that, in the end, the employees can act with individual responsibility. Nevertheless, the first line of defence against boreout has to be individual responsibility, for in many cases companies do not take their own responsibility as seriously as they should. So who is left in that case? You, and you alone.

We want to go a step further and pose a heretical question: is our doctrine of individual responsibility hollow?

Depending on the perspective taken, there are two opposing answers to this question. Let us first take a look at the negative response: the idea of individual responsibility has failed, since there is boreout.

It has failed if people suffer from boreout, survive by means of the various strategies and do not even take responsibility for addressing the problem themselves; if they persist in a condition of dissatisfaction instead of taking action and seeking out solutions; if they abuse the freedom offered by the company, which is extolled above all as the blessing of the 'new workplace'.

These employees shake the foundations on which a company is built.

It has also failed because, on the one hand, although many bosses are competent in their field of expertise they have had no preparation for their management role, and are therefore overstretched. While on the other hand, employees are mostly employees for just that reason, because free enterprise is really not for them and they are content to be directed by a guiding hand from above. It has failed, therefore, because the people involved and affected cannot deal properly with the free time they have in terms of their own individual responsibility.

The question once again: has the idea of individual responsibility failed? Let us turn to the positive side of the answer: no, it has not. Quite simply, there are no sensible alternatives. Nor is it possible to seriously imagine getting rid of the principle of individual responsibility, despite the problems connected with it, and returning to a 'planned economy workplace'. Moreover, we saw in the last chapter that checking on employees is really not a viable option, either in the setup of the workplace or in combating the boreout problem. Resorting to checks, however, would be one of the main consequences if we gave up on individual responsibility. But in fact the concept has not failed, even if some time often goes by before those affected by boreout wake from their lethargy and resolve to do something about the situation. It is the afflicted people who must act, and they will do so sooner or later.

Alex told a friend about boreout. She is head of a school, and studying at university at the same time. She sent Alex a message that illuminates boreout from a critical angle of individual responsibility.

Hello Alex,

I must make one thing clear: I do not suffer from boreout. I have not yet encountered this phenomenon, and I have worked as a waitress, a secretary and a teacher.

None of these jobs was a dream come true for me. They were all good at the time, and it was also great when I moved on to the next one. I am familiar with boring, monotonous, bureaucratic and unvalued tasks. I know about boredom, the lack of challenge and lack of motivation at work – and the mix of bad feelings that make you dissatisfied there. I know the discipline you have to find within yourself if you still want to get your job done.

But I do not know the boreout strategies you describe. I do not sink into my affliction. On the contrary: I love my work, it challenges me anew every day! And when something does not suit me, I change it. These boreout stories annoy me. This feeling sorry for yourself bores me. It's like the people who say they are 'trapped in the ditch between self-realization and the desire for prosperity and social esteem'. They dream of a vineyard and their own olive grove in Tuscany, then lean back casually, sighing. They know they are letting life slip away.

Let me make myself clear about this: I am no quixotic dreamer with hippie ideas. And I have no argument with capitalism, which 'leaves us all poor, some with money, others with dreams, blah blah'. Frankly, it is simple: boreout is a lazy excuse. It is basically a question of responsibility – respectable and boring. I maintain that anyone who has the courage to take responsibility for the lifestyle he or she has chosen will never suffer from boreout. Because understanding your own needs is part of taking responsibility for your own life, as is – if necessary – accepting the consequences and not hanging on in a crippling situation.

When you realize that your job is the wrong one, that you've made a wrong career choice, that you can learn nothing from your boss or achieve the goals that you find important – hey, why not accept the consequences? Of course it costs something – money, security or life ambitions. After all, we have known for a long time that money is not everything, that security is unobtainable anyway, and that our ambitions are not always realistic. Things do not always go further, higher and better. Life is not fair and nothing comes for free. For anyone. Because we cannot make life perfect, because it is bigger than we are, because we are at its mercy and must play the game according to its rules sooner or later.

I know the elements of boreout, but I do not know boreout as a phenomenon. So my answer to boreout is: change your job, or stay and sort yourself out. Don't moan about it. And if all else fails, you'll just have to lie on the bed you've made.

Clear words. The woman knows what she's talking about: the various elements of boreout, the boredom, the lack of challenges and the lack of involvement. The jobs she had were actually ideal breeding grounds for boreout. You might think she was repressing it. But we will not assume this. We are more optimistic: the individual elements of boredom – the under-stretching and demotivation – have not led to boreout in this case. Her description does not prove that boreout does not exist, but rather that it can be overcome or obviated. And, at the same time, she herself explains how she managed to do so: that is, by taking on her own individual responsibility.

10

Qualitative pay

There is a way out of boreout, and there is a way to avoid it. The basic principle of this is individual responsibility, as the previous chapter argued. Individual responsibility is, so to speak, our handbook for escaping from boreout. And so it is also the manual for our solution, which we call qualitative pay. Let us observe again, one male and one female worker (both affected by boreout), before we talk about recovery.

WORK AS A MILD ILLNESS

Diagnosis is the first step to recovery. We have covered this in the earlier chapters: we have seen what boreout is and how it arises. We have described how paradoxical the behaviour of affected people can be, and highlighted how stealthily boreout develops. Of course, we are not the first to identify boredom, under-stretching or lack of motivation in the workplace. Every element of boreout, taken individually, is well known. Nevertheless, with boreout we are describing a phenomenon that combines these three elements because they are mutually interdependent when they are present together and are complemented by the strategies – like an illness that exhibits a range of symptoms.

The German-American philosopher Frithjof Bergmann used precisely this simile. He called work a mild illness. As he remarks, a mild illness is quickly over, just like the working week: on Wednesday it is 'already' Wednesday, which helps in getting over Thursday and Friday. A masterly, absolutely spot-on comparison – especially in connection with boreout – which we would like to explore in this chapter on solutions. We see boreout as rather like influenza.

Fever, nausea or having a cold, none of symptoms in themselves amount to 'flu, assuming they appear individually. The 'flu diagnosis is only made when these symptoms appear in combination. This is the case with boreout: it is the combination of individual symptoms that leads to diagnosis of the boreout syndrome:

■ Boreout consists of three individual symptoms occurring in combination, as well as of the boreout strategies that are adopted: these are the individual component parts of boreout.

■ Because of the mutual interdependence of these component elements, a new syndrome emerges: boreout, which is the manifestation of the overall phenomenon.

In order to accommodate the multi-dimensionality of boreout, a solution is required that takes into account all of its elements.

What does that mean, exactly? Let us take a look at a concrete example. Theories about communications in the workplace often address the issue of how workers can get along better with their managers. You probably know the kind of advice that is offered, maybe from reading up on the subject or from hearing the cultural values that your company expounds: 'Address problems openly,' 'Give constructive feedback' and so on. This kind of approach offers a selective measure that would help, for example, if employees are understretched, and have the confidence to bring this up with their managers, who will no doubt give them more work to do as a result. That would solve this particular problem, but does not address the wider aspects of satisfaction in the workplace. And the problem may run deeper: what if the work doesn't interest these employees at all? Just getting more of the same will not make them happy. Thus we can see that a comprehensive approach is needed that takes into consideration the whole range of factors that influence satisfaction in the workplace. A superordinate procedure is needed in which the individual, short-term measures mentioned above are complemented by more wide-ranging solutions.

To come back to the comparison with 'flu: many medicines tackle only individual symptoms such as, for example, a runny nose. Taking a single medicine might help clear up the nose, but the 'flu would otherwise continue unabated.

There may be medicines that tackle a range of symptoms simultaneously. But they won't provide a cure in the absence of other measures – bed-rest, for example, is also needed. This combination of all the necessary measures, not just the use of individual medicines, is a basic principle of treatment that can provide an effective cure. And just as a range of measures is needed to cure 'flu, we must deploy a variety of elements in the struggle against boreout.

THE ELEMENTS OF QUALITATIVE PAY

We have seen that a multidimensional phenomenon requires a multidimensional solution. Our solution fulfils this criterion – it is what we call qualitative pay (Figure 10.1).

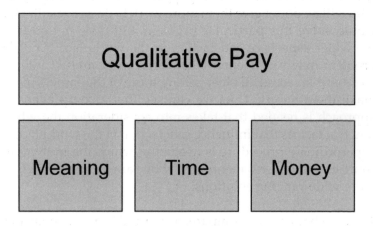

Figure 10.1   Aspects of qualitative pay

Meaning, time and money: these are, in our view, the central elements for satisfaction in the workplace. Bearing that in mind, let us look a little closer over the next few pages at what we understand by qualitative pay.

With the combination of these three elements we are expanding the concept of remuneration – away from the purely monetary meaning towards a comprehensive understanding. For you not only receive money for your work, but find personal satisfaction (the element of meaning) and are challenged. Moreover, if you are happy in your work, you will also make better use of your free time: feel more active, enjoy hobbies more intensively, and even find it fun to spend some of the money you have earned (the element of time).

This is the central point: qualitative pay is not defined by the absolute level of income, but rather is a mirror image of overall satisfaction with the workplace.

■ Qualitative pay is high when people are satisfied with all three elements, when they are sufficiently 'remunerated' in all three areas – not only monetarily.

■ Qualitative pay is low if contentment in these three areas is lacking or if there is a lack of balance (for example if the job provides great satisfaction but the pay is too low to support a decent standard of life).

■ Qualitative pay gives employees a sense of direction that helps to prevent boreout or, if they are already suffering, to defeat it. In this chapter we tend to talk of qualitative pay as a solution to existing problems, but let us point out here that it also helps to prevent boreout from arising in the first place.

■ The goal of the employees will be to maximize their personal, individual qualitative pay. Take care to avoid the trap of neglecting the less tangible aspects and focusing only on the question of pay. All three elements must be taken together and held in balance. Just as the elements of boreout mutually work upon each other, so too the three elements of qualitative pay must work together, as we have seen.

■ Qualitative pay involves a long-term strategy. It does not just mean a single measure taken in isolation to provide a short-term 'fix'; that may offer momentary relief, but it disregards long-term aspects and any benefits are soon whittled away. Real success depends on the combination of elements. Individual measures play a part in that, but they must be embedded in a lasting solution.

Each of the three elements is weighted at 40 per cent, making 120 per cent altogether. That is not a calculation error, but a symbolic indication that the whole is greater than the sum of the parts. It also means, of course, that none of the three elements plays a deciding role in providing fulfilment; each is in a minority when related to the whole.

As we have already stated, qualitative pay is a scheme that gives a sense of direction to help you find your way out of the boreout mess, or to prevent boreout in the first place. With this aim in mind, we will now take a closer look at each element of qualitative pay, and in each case give you tips about the future, boreout-free career path. The tips will help to maximize the benefits of work.

WE SEEK MEANING

Why exactly do we work? The off-the-cuff answer tends to be: because we have to, because we need money to live. It is primarily about purely ensuring one's existence and basic material needs.

Because we have to live, and because our standard of living is directly connected with money, we often ascribe too much weight to it. If the money is right, the job is right. We will put up with a lot in exchange for a good salary. Hence we often take on jobs that we don't in the least want to do. Not a very original conclusion, to be sure, but it is the truth nonetheless. Yet ask yourself: would the many employees in such situations stop working if they no longer had to because their basic needs were met – because they are simply rich? With respect, this is barely conceivable. In such a case, what would they do all day? Sit by the pool, go on a trip to the mountains or the Caribbean every so often and fill their stomachs like the lotus-eaters? Perhaps that would work for a short while, in the same way that a bit of boredom in the workplace for a short time has its attraction.

But, and this goes for the lotus-eaters too, you can have too much of a good thing. If we won the lottery, it would probably not be long before we were looking for something to do: maybe helping the couple next door to renovate their house, or maybe working for a charity or going back to college to develop our own ideas about some area of interest.

It is in cases of catastrophe that we see most starkly just how meaningful work can be: people help each other out in times of floods, landslides and earthquakes. Lives are saved, the sick cared for, emergency supplies shared out, money donated. Boreout is unthinkable in such situations. Or can you imagine people from the fire brigade or health workers turning their backs on the crisis and just lazing around?

So if we did not have to work because our material needs were covered, we would do so nonetheless. Our criteria for choosing what to do would, however, be different in this case: we could choose freely without having to consider the financial aspect. We would do what seems meaningful to us: what we like doing, what we find fun, something that we feel at ease with and identify with. The criteria would be the meanings we find in the work.

It is therefore not about having no work at all instead of an unloved job, but rather about meaningful work: something that provides us with satisfaction and recognition. It is through recognition that we find the meaning of what we do, because recognition gives us the feeling that we are real and that what we do is valued. When people praise us in our work, they recognize us. Whether in catastrophic situations or in everyday life, that gives us a meaning that is tangible and can be experienced.

The first element of qualitative pay is therefore meaning, for we must find it in our activities. If you do that you will find it easier to identify with your work, perhaps even find it fun. It is a question of looking for the meaning in what you do, or changing the basic conditions so that the meaning becomes clearer. This meaning is not simply present in the work; it exists in the relationship between work and worker. It must be discovered: by the bank clerk who develops strategies to make the business more profitable; by the police officer who wants to protect society from criminals; and by the doctor who helps the sick.

The point is this: what is meaningful for one person can be absolutely meaningless for another.

Think about whether your job at the moment is personally meaningful for you, about whether your work really interests you. First we must look at this idea we call 'interest'. Interest enables us to recognize the meaning of our activity very quickly for ourselves. The question 'Does my job really interest me?' is often suppressed, wrongly. For if interest in work is not present, then in all probability working days will become torment. Qualitative pay turns out to be higher if you are working at something that really interests you. For then you will spend your working time in satisfying ways.

> Work at something that really interests you.

The following list of questions can be a helpful aide memoire:

- Is the part of my work that interests me large enough?

- Do I go to work willingly?

■ Do I get enough recognition for what I do?

■ Is there another job that I would find much more exciting than my current work, and could I earn money doing that? Do I do such things, for example, in my free time?

■ Do I know people whose jobs I envy – not because they earn a lot but because they get exciting things to do? What makes me different from these people?

■ Did I choose my profession because it was what I wanted or because it was expected of me by my parents or teachers at the time?

First lesson: assign enough importance to interest. Frithjof Bergmann, mentioned above, says that most people do not do what really interests them. A sobering conclusion, but one that suggests that despite, or perhaps because of, the enormous number of job categories and profiles, it is not easy to find something you really want to do. Of course, what is also true is that not everyone can have interesting work. Many factors can prevent it – different gifts, a family to feed. And in our society there is an enormous amount of work that simply has to be done and that is just not interesting. But all the same, the question of interest, whenever possible, should be the compass by to which you orient yourself – either in looking at your current work or in considering a new job. Because if you can combine your personal interests with your work, then you have met a central precondition for maximizing your qualitative pay (in combination with the money and time elements).

As we have said, it is not granted to everyone to have work that really interests them. This makes it all the more important to take care of other factors that help give work meaning and can at least partly compensate for a lack of interest, because it is in just these necessary but tedious jobs that employees are most affected by boreout. In these cases, the approach should focus particularly on the interpersonal level, on communication. That can help show why the tasks are necessary and so give them meaning. Active communication can help you to better see how your role fits into the context of the wider organization. And by communicating, you can show that you take an interest in the organization and that you are ready for challenging, demanding activities.

Discover the meaning of your work by actively communicating.

Many activities are meaningful, even if the meaning is not always so obvious such as in the care sector. In these cases, it is necessary to communicate this meaning. This is too often ignored in the normal work routine.

For example, managers tend to hand out particular tasks to their employees without bothering to explain what the purpose is or what the work will achieve. The employees have to carry out the task without seeing the larger context, let alone understanding it. Then there are the managers who never delegate the interesting tasks and hence offer their staff too few opportunities to carry out meaningful work. This may seem well enough on the surface, but over the long term work becomes less and less meaningful and the employees begin to lose interest in what they are doing.

For this reason, you need to engage actively in the question and try to identify the meaning of your work. The following list of questions can be helpful here:

■   Begin with yourself: do I see the meaning in my work, even if it does not interest me that much?

- If not, how can I get my boss to explain the meaning of my work to me?

- Is there meaningful work within my company that I don't get to take part in? Could I change that by talking to someone higher up?

- Do I make it obvious to everyone who matters in the company that I am interested in meaningful work – or do I give the impression of being lazy or unmotivated?

- How can I show that I am interested in the company and see meaning in its activity, but let people know that in my daily routine I do not get enough meaningful work to do?

Our mantra is individual responsibility. You are right if you now protest that at this point we have come up against the boundary of individual responsibility. Communication is always two-way, so you always have to depend on the person on the other side. If your manager does not respond to your signals, then at a certain point you can't do any more. Here it is also important that your boss takes the time to address you and your concerns; excuses like 'Don't have any time, I'm under a lot of pressure' are OK once or twice, but not permanently.

Your last resort is, of course, to hand in your notice. Before you do that, though, you should do everything you can to resolve your problems, because otherwise you are likely to slide into the same slough of despondency in another location.

The third approach for recognizing meaning in work is related to your personal attitude to it. You might be able to do more to feel good at work and to discover the meaning in your daily activity. A positive general mental attitude makes you ready for new and unexpected things, and opens up many more opportunities than a morose 'get away from me' grumbling.

> **Work on your attitude to work.**

This is especially about how you can motivate yourself to be able to perform the less interesting tasks with at least a positive basic attitude. Positive thinking is just as much a part of this as fun. Stephen Lundin and his co-authors have composed a fascinating contribution to this topic. Their book *Fish* provides four simple mantras that, among other things, can alleviate the problems we have portrayed. They are: 'Choose your attitude', 'Games', 'Be a joy to others' and 'Be present'. Their credo: you can find satisfaction even in boring and meaningless work if only your attitude is right. And you can influence this.

We are of the firm opinion that a fully developed game culture makes the workplace considerably more bearable than does the dusty, card-index culture of many insurance companies, banks and government departments. Look out for opportunities to increase your satisfaction at work. For example, it is fun to give pleasure to others. Do not mis-understand us: these and similar motivational approaches often cannot conceal the fact that a lot of work is still boring and repetitive. But they can make the mild illness of work more bearable. And the key to that is to encourage the em-ployee to look for meaning not simply in the individual activity, but in the workplace as a whole.

A good working atmosphere cannot make dull work more interesting, but it can make it more bearable. And perhaps, if you maintain a positive mental attitude, new opportunities and a chance of work that really interests you will result.

We can also look at it from the opposite viewpoint: a job that is potentially very exciting can quickly be turned into misery by narrow-minded and repellent colleagues. A rigid, unsophisticated and boring culture can ruin even the brightest prospects. If you start working in such an environment, you will very soon become aware of both the overt and covert dynamics of office politics as they play out, and you will probably find them very depressing. The joy and interest in your profession will evaporate – then it is time for a U-turn.

To sum up: these approaches are aimed specifically at conquering lack of interest by finding meaning. So try to recognize the meaning in your work by means of the techniques just described. If your work is interesting, so much the better. If not, make use of the suggestions to find at least a little bit of meaning in your work and to make the 'mild illness' more bearable. Life is too short – and working life too long – to be constantly living with the knowledge that you are doing something you find meaningless.

But do not despair over the question of meaning. If your work bores you intensely and all your efforts fail to reveal anything of interest in it, and if your boss does not respond to your suggestions or the working atmosphere is poisonous, then you must act as quickly as possible:

> Give your notice when you have finally had enough of the blatant meaninglessness of your work.

If you simply cannot get ahead in your workplace, then leave; do not just surrender to a boreout fate. For no one, least of all you yourself, is helped by your being dissatisfied in your workplace and dragging this dissatisfaction into your free time. And when you are looking for a new job, make it something you consider meaningful. Otherwise you are going out of the frying pan into the fire. Change will do nothing if you are still fundamentally doing the wrong sort of work, unless of course the problem is simply a case of being in the wrong location (as described in the chapter on causes). In that case, a change of location may be the answer. But if you are in the wrong career or the wrong field of work, you need a fundamentally new start. This may take longer to accomplish – but will be a much more lasting change when you have made it.

You see, meaningful work is of central importance for long-lasting professional contentment. If we get the most out of it, then our qualitative pay increases. But a word of caution: that is only one part of the wider picture, for even those people with interesting jobs can be bored or understretched or earn too little. Focusing just on meaning to the exclusion of other factors does not solve the boreout problem. Let us therefore turn to the second element of qualitative pay: time.

WE VALUE TIME

Time is money. That is a well-known saying, but also rather one-dimensional. For time is much more than this: it is our most valuable asset. You only have one lifetime, so you need to handle it wisely and be clear about what you want to spend your time doing and where your own priorities lie. The value of time is shown with age. Older people only want one thing: time with the people they would like to spend it with.

Time, as we understand it with regard to qualitative pay, is related on the one hand to the amount of time that the employee dedicates to work (quantitative), which is by no means trivial. Including travel to and from work, the average employee spends 9 or 10 hours a day on work-related activity.

What remains after that is free time. It is important to create a clear distinction between that and the time that you spend at work. You should be able to switch off and turn to those people and things that are really important to you. (We have to admit, however, that many people today do not really know what they want to do with their free time.) Do not confuse this free time with the free time at work that those affected by boreout have at their disposal. They can certainly use this time for personal matters (see the chapter on strategies), but, as we have seen, after a certain period of time they no longer feel comfortable with this. Our topic here is the genuine free time outside working hours. On the one hand, we are dealing with the question of how much time we dedicate to work and how much to ourselves. This is about getting the right balance between the two: the time given up to work should not become too dominant, because otherwise we will miss out on the free time we need.

So far, we have been talking about time in quantitative terms. Now we want to consider another aspect, what we might call 'qualitative' time. This relates to the way employees spend their time at work and what they do when they are there. We know that when we have too little to do, we are understretched and begin to get bored. Here, we run up almost head-on against these important causes of boreout.

Our first tip for using time in a satisfying way relates to the qualitative element:

> Seek out work during working hours.

That may sound rather pathetic. But nonetheless, a person affected by boreout does need to ask for work in order to have something to do during working hours. You must aim to have enough work to occupy your time, so that you are actually doing something constructive. Above all, see this through the lens of the boreout paradox. The prospect of sweet idleness seems seductive at first glance, and it may seem absurd to be asking for work when you might instead have some time to yourself (during work). But if you begin to do nothing over long periods, that is where you begin to be trapped in the vicious circle of boreout.

The way to get more to do is to ask for it. You must be prepared to break out of the boreout cycle and to do without all the strategies that keep work at arm's length. You must be prepared to renounce the supposedly sweet idleness and to search for ways of occupying yourself that actually have something to do with your work. If you have come so far, then you can discuss the topic with your boss – a difficult but necessary step.

The following tips can help with this discussion:

- ■ Don't sound confrontational. You may be tempted to tell the boss exactly what you think, but here you have to focus on what you want to achieve: your aim is to get sufficient, and satisfying, work for yourself, not to give the boss a piece of your mind.

- ■ A critical faculty is a rare gift. Formulate your concern as a request ('I would like…') and not as a criticism ('It's bad that I don't…').

- ■ Say openly and clearly that you have too little to do, and communicate your desire to work more and to take on more responsibility.

- ■ Demonstrate beforehand that you can do it. Devise something without being asked that you can put forward during the discussion. Sort out something in advance that will help you in the discussion. In this way, show that you are capable of more, that you know more and that you can achieve more than is currently expected of you.

■ Make your boss aware of the need to delegate more and not always do everything alone, especially the interesting things. If he or she believes no one else on the team is up to the challenging tasks, give yourself the chance to demonstrate otherwise.

In most cases, such a discussion will open your boss's eyes, and you are likely to be given not just more work, but also work that is more meaningful and interesting. Notice again the importance of the relationship between meaning and time: you gain nothing if the boss simply gives you a greater quantity of work that is boring, meaningless and un-challenging, like filing or adjusting the prices in the product catalogue (something that no one likes doing but that has to be done some time).

If your boss takes this discussion the wrong way and only burdens you with meaningless activities, or continues to treat you as the office idiot despite your openness and honesty, then the moment has come for you to act quickly and decisively. If your boss seems to show willing but cannot do anything about the situation, then you will have to face the facts. If the prospect before you is one of constant understretch and boredom, even though you have tried to talk things through and have proved that you want to do and can do more, then you must go.

Give your notice if you want nothing more to do with blatant boredom and understretching.

Let us now come back to the quantitative aspect of time. This goes beyond the actual time spent at work and has to do with your free time as well. You must find a balance between the time that you give to work and the time that you have at your own free disposal.

Seek and find the right balance between working time and free time.

Qualitative pay is also increased if you have enough time to be able to actually enjoy the money you have earned: eating out with your partner, developing friendships, having time for sport, music and travel. That is what you work for, after all: to satisfy your needs outside the workplace (you only need the money for your non-working hours). By the way, this can lead to another ridiculous paradox: the more you work and the further you go professionally, the more you will earn, all things being equal. And the less you will get from the money, because you spend most of your time in the workplace.

Think back for a moment to the pseudo-commitment strategy, which can lead to the following thoroughly grotesque situation: an employee spends as much time in the office as the boss, in order to display stress and single-minded commitment at the same time. But if the truth be known, such employees are sitting all alone and getting bored. What they do above all, however, is to cut down on their real free time, because they assume that that is what the boss expects of them. Whoever stays the longest while doing the least wins. This employee remains in the workplace far longer than is necessary, and fails to achieve any remotely satisfactory work–life balance.

You must be careful not to let the balance tilt too heavily in favour of work. Do not add to your working hours unnecessarily. You will only lose by it, and no one will gain.

Finally, we need to look at the option of part-time work. In the past 20 years a multitude of new work–life patterns have evolved, which increasingly blur and adapt the boundaries between work and free time. These are not simply work models but also actual life models. They are often based on a comprehensive view of a lifetime as a whole and do not focus merely on work. Such models have two advantages: on the one hand, they increase the proportion of free time. On the other, they reduce the proportion of the time during which you have to confront the mild illness of work. This allows many people to compensate for a lack of achievement and interest at work with more free time or greater flexibility in carrying out their jobs.

> ### Choose a different work–life model.

Make a decision to work, for example, only 80 per cent of the normal day, if your company offers that option. Cut back your time at work and take more time for yourself. It might be just this 20 per cent that can make the difference and prevent your work from becoming an illness in the first place. Another possibility: you could work from home, which allows you to be with your children, to eat with your partner or simply to live according to your own working rhythm.

At this point we would like once again to emphasize the following points: these work–life models do not eliminate the boreout problem in the workplace. You can still get bored, be understretched and be unmotivated in the workplace. But at least you reduce the proportion of your life that you spend in the office.

If this and similar approaches seem to offer you something, then take them on board. At this point we draw attention once again to Frithjof Bergmann and his approach to the 'new work', which at its core is responsive to boreout and the fact that most people spend too much time on things that do not interest them. Part-time work models and alternative occupations are the solution, in Bergmann's view. His approach may seem somewhat utopian, but he aptly describes the idea of looking for a balance between different activities.

WE DESIRE MONEY

The final element of qualitative pay is money: the salary you obtain for putting up with the mild illness of work and selling your time to the company. This element has no direct relation to boreout, but it is the primary motivation for people to work. It is also an indispensable element in managing to survive. Money allows you to take advantage of the consumer world and to satisfy your various needs and desires: eating and drinking, holidays, a nice car, a DVD player and much more. Money makes life easier and nicer; it does not make everything possible – but a lot, nonetheless. Please note that we are not arguing that you should turn your back on money. There are approaches that praise austerity – we are no fans of these. On the contrary, we think, quite simply, that money is great.

But how high should this pay be, ideally? The instinctive answer is, of course: as high as possible.

Get the very best pay deal you can!

This instinct to look for the best possible deal is basically correct: you should never undersell yourself. Why be satisfied with less when you can get more? The danger lies in the tendency to think that nothing matters except making as much money as possible. That tendency neglects the other elements that are just as important for personal contentment – and not just in the workplace. Yes, money is great. But it is also a deceiver, because is makes us believe that we would be happy if we only had plenty of it. But at the precise moment when you have a lot of it, money and the things you can buy with it often quickly lose their charm. Surveys reveal this again and again. And money, too, has its price. Anyone who is oriented solely towards money and leaves meaning and time out of the equation will pay in dissatisfaction, frustration, loss of friendships and even health problems. Hence money is a poor criterion for the choice of work; in itself, if it overrides other needs, it may not be able to compensate for dissatisfaction. It can even become an obstacle to doing what you really want to do.

Nevertheless, maximize your monetary remuneration. Ask for a pay rise, compare your salary to that of your colleagues. You can even change jobs if you will earn more in another location, but in so doing remember the elements of meaning and time. If you are trapped in the wrong job, then all the money in the world will not help you to spend your working days in contentment.

TO SUMMARIZE

Consider qualitative pay as a vehicle that enables you to avoid boreout (prevention) or to escape from it (recovery). Analyse your situation by applying the new weightings and keep the three criteria of meaning, time and money in view.

Never decide one-dimensionally, and do not throw away something that you will later regret. That rarely works. We would congratulate you if the lack of meaning in your work seems unimportant when set against the money you earn. We would also congratulate you if you could do almost entirely without money for the sake of the meaning of your work. Leading workers in banks and insurance companies arguably belong in the first group, relief organization workers and monks in the second. If you fall into neither of these categories, then you must factor all three elements into your calculations.

And once again: ask yourself early on in your life whether what you are doing or plan to do really interests you. Do not allow yourself to be over-influenced by external factors (friends and family). If you are in a profession that seems to have no meaning, think about that first, before you leave the company in frustration. Not everyone finds everything equally meaningful: listen to yourself and not to the others. Work on your attitude, because that is central: if, from the very beginning, you are going to work reluctantly, it is obvious that you do not see the meaning in it. Fun helps. Work on the game culture in your team, without letting that lead you to become unreliable or negligent. Only if all else fails should you go. But consider carefully whether you are just in the wrong location, or whether you have simply chosen the wrong kind of career. In the second case a move to a similar post would do you little or no good. Then you would have to consider whether something in your career path needs to change more fundamentally.

If you have answered the meaning question, you should ensure that you are also able to do meaningful work. It is no use for you to find an apparently exciting position or to have chosen a seemingly glamorous career path if you are not then engaged in interesting work and spend hours on end with nothing to do. Never neglect the qualitative aspect of time. Really fill your time at work with challenging content.

Remember too the quantitative side of time: as the saying goes, 'too much work makes Jack a dull boy.' Too much of a good thing is definitely too much. A proper balance of a reasonable time at work with enough freedom for your private life helps you in finding your own personal fulfilment. Make sure you have enough time to meet your personal needs.

Finally, do not neglect your salary. Money is important, and not just to secure your basic needs. It makes you more independent. Do not neglect this aspect. Get the best deal you can for yourself, without, however, forgetting the elements of meaning and time, for that is your greatest danger here. Focusing on money alone is poor strategy.

Your qualitative pay is high if you get enough of all three elements, in which case the overall reward is large. Your qualitative pay is low if you fail to do so. In that case the chance of boreout is high. The classic example: you are doing something that does not interest you (lacking meaning), are bored and understretched because you have too little to do (poor quality of time), but are earning well (high salary), and so put up with things. In this combination you would need to make a very great effort to get yourself out of the situation.

Put your qualitative pay glasses on from the very beginning. That will help you to avoid boreout. If you are already in a boreout mess, go through our tips and attempt to improve the way you operate in your workplace. If all that fails, then hand in your notice. Risk making a new beginning. But please, do everything you can to make sure it is the right new beginning. Do not forget our glasses, to help you see things clearly...

Closing thoughts

Let us end this excursion into the world of work in the 21st century with some good news and some bad news.

First the bad news: we have another problem. To add to bullying, burnout and postural deformities caused by ergonomically bad working positions, we have come up with a new diagnosis. Boreout destroys the illusion of general happiness in the workplace that is promised to us in every further education course, by every careers advisor and in every job advertisement. It is also responsible for the bad feeling that afflicts us when we think about work. Perhaps, after reading this book, you are getting wise to that bad feeling, perhaps at least it amuses you to identify it in others. But those are all just consolations that help to deal with this new phenomenon in some way.

And now we come to the good news. We can solve the problem – and the individualization of our society can help us to get rid of boreout. Becoming aware of your own situation and your own needs is part of individualization. In concrete terms, that means that we no longer simply put up with everything that happens to us at work. We do not give in to our fate, but rather we demand more from our occupation. We do this in two respects: in terms of content, because we are looking for fulfilment of a sense of meaning; and formally, because we wish to be well reimbursed for our work, because we have high expectations of our working environment and because we want manageable working hours.

Do not allow yourself to be misled by the oh-so-scientific experts, who are always saying that work may not and cannot be fun (for everyone). Forget that. In our individualized society there are still many other things to which not everyone is entitled, or that would no longer function if everyone laid claim to them.

Seek single-mindedly the best result for yourself at work. And try too to find meaning and fulfilment in your work. For, despite all the prophecies of doom, there is still more to work than just earning money. Individualization makes it possible to identify and feed our other needs and desires. In it lies the solution we have identified – what we call qualitative pay. It is true that you can put up with a low level of qualitative pay for a certain period of time – and so, doing a job that perhaps no one else wants, you may feel you at least make a contribution to the economy. But that does not mean you can go on and on without fulfilment or a sense of meaning in your work – you only put up with losses over a certain period of time. And it also does not mean that you should not strive for an improvement in your situation.

Boreout – as we have already emphasized several times – is a phenomenon that differs from individual to individual. Not everyone is understretched, unmotivated or bored out in the same situation. People find fulfilment or a sense of meaning in different activities. And everyone affected must find their own way to deal with problems in the workplace. In so doing, we should learn to ignore social judgements and to listen to our own inner voice. That also goes for questions about our situation in the workplace. We decide for ourselves about where we find satisfaction, what work we consider meaningful and which solution we will use to combat boreout. For this reason, boreout is not simply a problem – but also a chance for perfecting individualization.

Bibliography

Adams, Scott (1997) *The Dilbert Principle: A cubicle's eye view of bosses, meetings, management fads and other workplace afflictions*, Boxtree Limited

Bergmann, Frithjof (2004) *Neue Arbeit, neue Kultur*, Arbor Verlag (*New Work, New Culture*)

Brothers Grimm (1995), Hans in Luck, in: *Grimm's Fairy Tales*, Penguin Classics

Cobaugh, Heike M and Schwerdtfeger, Susanne (2003) *Work–Life-Balance*, Redline Wirtschaft

Csikszentmihalyi, Mihaly (2000) *Beyond Boredom and Anxiety: Experiencing flow in work and play*, Jossey-Bass

Csikszentmihalyi, Mihaly (2002) *Flow: The classic work on how to achieve happiness*, Rider and Co

Dehner, Ulrich (2004) *Die alltäglichen Spielchen im Büro*, Piper Verlag (*Everyday Little Office Games*)

De Sadeleer, Luke and Sherren, Joseph (2001) *Vitamin C for a Healthy Workplace*, www.creativebound.com

Englert, Sylvia (2003) *Das ist mein Job*, Econ (*That is my job*)

Kaye, Beverly and Jordan-Evans, Sharon (2005) *Love It, Don't Leave It*, Gabal Verlag,

Lundin, Stephen C, Paul, Harry and Christensen, John (2003) *Fish! A remarkable way to boost morale and improve results,* Coronet Books

Maier, Corinne (2005) *Hello Laziness! Why hard work doesn't pay,* Orion

Maslach, Christina and Leiter, Michael P (1997) *The Truth about Burnout,* Jossey-Bass

Merg, Klaus/Knödler, Torsten (2005) *Überleben im Job,* Redline Wirtschaft *(Surviving in a Job)*

ARTICLES/SURVEYS

Gallup Organization (2004–2006) Engagement Index: Studie zur Messung der emotionalen Bindung von MitarbeiterInnen, Untersuchungen von

Irle, Mathias (2005) Schluss mit lustig. Macht Ihnen Ihre Arbeit Spaß? Nein? Nicht schlimm! Alles andere wäre eine Ausnahme, Sagt der St. Galler Professor Fredmund Malik, in: *brand eins, Wirtschaftsmagazin,* 7, September, 70–71.

Kelly Services (2005a) Contentment in the workplace, www.kellyservices.com, June

Kelly Services (2005b) Ethics in the workplace, www.kellyservices.com, September

Kelly Services (2005c) Stress in the workplace, www.kellyservices.com, November

Malachowski, Dan (for galaxy.com and AOL) (2005) *Wasted time at work costing companies billions,* www.salary.com/careers/layouthtmls/crel_display_nocat_Ser374_Par555.html, July

Possemeyer, Ines and Killmeyer, Franz (2005) Gesellschaft in Zeitnot; Die Diktatur der Uhr, *GEO,* August

Saavedra, Mario (2005) 8 horas sin intimidad: Así nos espían en nuestro trabajo, *CNR,* November

Index

NB: page numbers in *italics* indicate figures and tables in the text

3 1170 00789 2080